INDULGENCE FOOD

RECIPE DEVELOPMENT
Penny Cox, Donna Hay,
Elise Pascoe, Anna Phillips

EDITORIAL
US Editor: Anna Brandenburger
Food Editor: Sheryle Eastwood
Assistant Food Editor: Anneka Mitchell
Home Economist: Donna Hay
Editorial Coordinator: Margaret Kelly

PHOTOGRAPHY
Andrew Payne

STYLING
Rosemary De Santis

COVER DESIGN
Frank Pithers

DESIGN AND PRODUCTION
Manager: Nadia Sbisa
Senior Production Editor: Rachel Blackmore
Design and Layout: Margie Mulray
Finished Art: Chris Hatcher

PUBLISHER
Philippa Sandall

Published by J.B. Fairfax Press Inc.,
a wholly owned subsidiary of J.B. Fairfax International

Includes Index
ISBN 1 56197 021 2
Formatted by J.B. Fairfax Press Pty Ltd
Printed by Toppan Printing Co, Hong Kong

CONTENTS

MICROWAVE IT

Where microwave instructions occur in this book a microwave oven with a 650 watt output has been used. Wattage on domestic microwave ovens varies between 500 and 700 watts, so it may be necessary to vary the cooking times slightly depending on the wattage of your oven.

CHECK-AND-GO

Use the easy Check-and-Go boxes which appear beside each ingredient. Simply check your pantry and if the ingredients are not there, tick the boxes as a reminder to add those items to your shopping list.

CANNED FOODS

Can sizes vary between countries and manufacturers. You may find the quantities in this book are slightly different to what is available. Purchase and use the can size nearest to the suggested size in the recipe.

METRIC CUPS & SPOONS

Metric	Cups	Imperial
60 mL	$1/4$ cup	2 fl oz
80 mL	$1/3$ cup	$2^1/2$ fl oz
120 mL	$1/2$ cup	4 fl oz
240 mL	1 cup	8 fl oz
	Spoons	
1.25 mL	$1/4$ teaspoon	
2.5 mL	$1/2$ teaspoon	
5 mL	1 teaspoon	
15 mL	1 tablespoon	

WICKEDLY DELICIOUS

Devoted to delicious desserts and cakes, this chapter
looks elaborate but, even so, don't think that everything in it
is hard to make. All the recipes are simple to follow and with
a little care your efforts will look just like the photographs.

CHOCOLATE MUD CAKE WITH CHOCOLATE SAUCE

*Whatever the occasion for
the true chocoholic, this cake with
its rich chocolate sauce is a
party in itself.*

Serves 10-12
Oven temperature 250°F (120°C)

- [ ] 9 oz (250 g) butter, chopped
- [ ] 10¹/₂ oz (300 g) semi-sweet chocolate
- [ ] 5 eggs, separated
- [ ] 2 tablespoons sugar
- [ ] 3 tablespoons self-rising flour, sifted
- [ ] whipped cream

RICH CHOCOLATE SAUCE
- [ ] 7 oz (200 g) semi-sweet chocolate, broken into small pieces
- [ ] 2¹/₂ oz (75 g) unsalted butter
- [ ] ³/₄ cup (180 mL) sugar
- [ ] 4 tablespoons cocoa powder, sifted
- [ ] ¹/₄ cup (60 mL) milk
- [ ] ¹/₄ cup (60 mL) heavy cream

1   Place butter and chocolate in top of a double boiler and heat over simmering water, stirring until melted and smooth. Remove top pan and allow chocolate mixture to cool slightly.

2   Beat egg yolks and sugar into chocolate mixture then fold through flour.

3   Place egg whites in a mixing bowl and beat until stiff peaks form. Fold lightly into chocolate mixture. Pour into a greased and lined 8-inch round cake pan. Bake for 1¹/₄ hours, or until cooked when tested with a skewer. Turn off oven and cool cake in oven with door ajar.

4   To make sauce, place chocolate and butter in top of double boiler and heat over simmering water until melted. Stir in sugar and cocoa powder and mix to combine. Add milk and cream and heat for 5 minutes longer, stirring occasionally. Remove pan from heat and pour sauce into a jug. Set aside to cool. Serve cake with sauce and cream.

Chocolate Mud Cake with Chocolate Sauce

BERRY STACKS

Serves 6
Oven temperature 375°F (190°C)

- [ ] **2 egg whites**
- [ ] **$1/2$ cup (120 mL) sugar**
- [ ] **4 tablespoons butter, melted and cooled**
- [ ] **$1/2$ cup (120 mL) all-purpose flour, sifted**
- [ ] **1 tablespoon dark rum**
- [ ] **confectioners sugar**

FILLING
- [ ] **1 egg, lightly beaten**
- [ ] **3 tablespoons sugar**
- [ ] **$1^1/2$ tablespoons cornstarch**
- [ ] **1 teaspoon vanilla extract**
- [ ] **$2/3$ cup (160 mL) milk, scalded**
- [ ] **1 tablespoon butter**
- [ ] **1 cup (240 mL) heavy cream, whipped**
- [ ] **1 pint small strawberries, hulled and halved**

- [ ] **$3/4$ pint blueberries**

RASPBERRY COULIS
- [ ] **1 pint raspberries**
- [ ] **1 tablespoon sugar**
- [ ] **2 tablespoons Framboise (raspberry liqueur)**

1 Beat egg whites until soft peaks form. Add sugar a little at a time, beating well after each addition. Beat until sugar dissolves and mixture is thick and glossy. Add butter and beat. Fold through flour and rum.

2 Place spoonfuls of mixture onto a greased and lined cookie sheet and spread to form thin $3^1/2$-inch (7.5 cm) circles. Bake for 6-8 minutes, or until a light golden color. Allow to cool on trays.

3 To make filling, combine egg, sugar, cornstarch and vanilla extract in a saucepan. Whisk in milk and stir over a low heat until mixture is smooth and thickens. Beat in butter and set aside to cool, then fold through cream.

4 To make coulis, place raspberries, sugar and liqueur in a food processor or blender and process until smooth.

5 To assemble, place a cookie circle on each serving plate, spoon a little filling over and top with strawberries and blueberries. Repeat layers using four cookie circles, finishing with a cookie circle. Serve with coulis. Dust with sifted confectioners sugar.

BERRY CHARLOTTE

Serves 6

- [ ] **9 lady fingers**
- [ ] **9 cigarette wafers**

FILLING
- [ ] **16 tablespoons unsalted butter, softened**
- [ ] **$3/4$ cup (180 mL) sugar**
- [ ] **2 tablespoons dark rum**
- [ ] **$1^2/3$ cup (410 mL) ground almonds**
- [ ] **$1^1/4$ cups (300 mL) heavy cream**
- [ ] **16 oz (440 g) canned blackberries,**

COOK'S TIP

Fresh blackberries and boysen-berries make the Berry Charlotte even more indulgent. If using fresh berries use 2 cups (250 g) blackberries and 2 cups (250 g) boysenberries.

China Limoges *Silverwear* Oneida

drained
- [ ] **16 oz (440 g) canned boysenberries, drained**

1   Arrange lady fingers and cigarette wafers alternately around the sides of a greased and foil-lined 7-inch (18 cm) springform pan, trimming bottom end of lady fingers to fit if necessary.

2   To make filling, beat butter and sugar until light and fluffy. Add rum and ground almonds and beat well. Whip cream until soft peaks form. Fold through almond mixture.

3   Spoon one-third of mixture into prepared pan and arrange drained blackberries evenly over top. Spoon another third of mixture over black-berries and top evenly with drained boysenberries. Spoon remaining mixture over boysenberries. Refrigerate over-night or until firm. To serve, remove from pan and arrange on a serving platter. Tie ribbon decoratively around outside of charlotte.

Plate Incorporated Agencies

🍓
BLISSFUL BOMBE

Serves 12

VANILLA ICE CREAM
- [ ] **1 cup (240 mL) sugar**
- [ ] **8 egg yolks**
- [ ] **2²/₃ cups (650 mL) light cream**
- [ ] **1 vanilla bean**
- [ ] **1¹/₂ cups (355 mL) heavy cream**

CHOCOLATE MOUSSE
- [ ] **6 oz (175 g) semi-sweet chocolate, chopped**
- [ ] **3 tablespoons strong black coffee**
- [ ] **4 eggs, separated**
- [ ] **1 tablespoon butter, softened**
- [ ] **1 tablespoon brandy**
- [ ] **3 tablespoons sugar**
- [ ] **¹/₂ cup (120 mL) heavy cream, whipped**

1   To make ice cream, place sugar and egg yolks in a bowl and beat until thick and creamy. Place light cream and vanilla bean in a heavy-based saucepan and

Left: Berry Stacks, Berry Charlotte
Above: Blissful Bombe

simmer for 3 minutes. Cool slightly, then remove vanilla bean.

2   Gradually add 1 cup (240 mL) of warm cream to egg mixture, beating well. Add egg mixture to remaining cream, stirring over low heat until mixture coats the back of a spoon. Set aside to cool.

3   Stir through heavy cream, pour into a freezerproof tray lined with plastic wrap, and freeze until almost set. Break up mixture with a fork and place in food processor. Process until mixture is thick and creamy. Pour ice cream into a chilled mould (9 cup/2.25 liter capacity) lined with plastic wrap. Push a smaller mould, covered with plastic wrap, into center of ice cream, forcing ice cream up around the sides of the mould. Freeze until firm.

4   To make chocolate mousse, place chocolate and coffee in a bowl and melt over hot water, stirring until smooth. Remove from heat and beat in egg yolks one at a time. Continue beating and add butter and brandy. Allow mixture to cool.

5   Beat egg whites until soft peaks form, then beat in sugar. Fold egg whites and cream through chocolate mixture. Remove smaller mould from ice cream. Spoon mousse into center of ice cream and return to freezer until set.

❦

STRIPED ROULADE WITH APRICOT MOUSSE FILLING

This impressive roulade may look very grand but it is in fact easy to make. Follow our step-by-step recipe and see just how easy it really is.

Serves 6
Oven temperature 400°F (200°C)

- ☐ ¹/₂ cup (120 mL) self-rising flour, sifted
- ☐ 2 tablespoons cocoa, sifted
- ☐ 4 eggs
- ☐ 5 tablespoons sugar

APRICOT MOUSSE FILLING
- ☐ 1 tablespoon unflavored gelatin
- ☐ 3 tablespoons apricot nectar
- ☐ 16 oz (440 g) canned apricots, drained and 3 tablespoons liquid reserved
- ☐ 3 eggs, separated
- ☐ ¹/₄ cup (60 mL) sugar
- ☐ 1 tablespoon brandy
- ☐ 1 tablespoon Cointreau
- ☐ ¹/₂ cup (120 mL) heavy cream

1   Place 2 tablespoons flour and cocoa in a mixing bowl and the remaining flour in another.
2   Beat eggs and sugar until thick and creamy. Divide mixture evenly between two bowls. Fold cocoa mixture through egg mixture in one bowl and fold flour mixture through the remaining egg mixture.
3   Place chocolate and plain cake batters into two separate piping bags fitted with ¹/₂-inch (1.5 cm) plain nozzles. Pipe lines of chocolate mixture ¹/₂-inch (1.5 cm) apart diagonally across a greased and lined jelly roll pan. Then pipe plain mixture in lines between chocolate strips. Bake for 8-10 minutes, or until cake is cooked through and springy to touch.
4   Turn roulade out onto a damp kitchen towel sprinkled with sugar. Roll up with kitchen towel from short end and allow to cool.
5   To make filling, sprinkle gelatin over apricot nectar in a small bowl, place it over a small saucepan of simmering water and stir until gelatin dissolves. Set aside to cool at room temperature. Place apricots and reserved liquid in a food processor or blender and process until smooth. Beat egg yolks and sugar in a bowl until thick

and creamy. Stir in apricot purée, gelatin mixture, brandy and Cointreau. Beat cream until soft peaks form, fold into apricot mixture. Beat egg whites until soft peaks form, fold into apricot mixture. Refrigerate for 2-3 hours, or until mixture is almost set. Unroll roulade and spread with filling. Reroll and refrigerate until filling is set.

Pipe lines of chocolate mixture ¹/₂-inch (1.5 cm) apart diagonally across a greased and lined jelly roll pan. Then pipe plain mixture between chocolate stripes.

Turn roulade onto a damp kitchen towel sprinkled with sugar, and roll up from short end.

Unroll roulade, spread with filling, and reroll. Refrigerate until filling is set.

Props Accoutrement

9

China Limoges *Silverware* Oneida

CHOCOLATE
MERINGUE CAKE

Serves 10
Oven temperature 250°F (120°C)

HAZELNUT MERINGUE
- ☐ 1¼ cup (300 mL) hazelnuts, ground
- ☐ 2 tablespoons cornstarch
- ☐ 1¼ cups (300 mL) sugar
- ☐ 6 egg whites
- ☐ whipped cream

CHOCOLATE FILLING
- ☐ 16 tablespoons unsalted butter
- ☐ 6½ oz (185 g) semi-sweet chocolate, melted
- ☐ 3 tablespoons sugar
- ☐ 2 cups (470 mL) cream
- ☐ 2 tablespoons brandy
- ☐ 1 cup (240 mL) hazelnuts, ground

CHOCOLATE TOPPING
- ☐ 5 oz (155 g) semi-sweet chocolate
- ☐ 2 teaspoons vegetable oil

1   To make meringue, mix together ground hazelnuts, cornstarch and ³/₄ cup (180 mL) sugar. Beat egg whites until soft peaks form, add remaining sugar a little at a time and beat until thick and glossy. Fold into hazelnut mixture.

2   Mark three 8-inch (20 cm) squares on parchment paper and place on cookie sheets. Place meringue mixture in a piping bag fitted with a small plain nozzle and pipe mixture to outline squares, then fill centers with piped lines of mixture. Bake for 40-50 minutes, or until crisp and dry.

3   To make filling, beat butter until soft. Add chocolate, sugar and cream and beat until thick. Fold in brandy and hazelnuts.

4   To make topping, place chocolate and oil in the top of a double boiler and heat over simmering water, stirring until chocolate melts and mixture is smooth. Remove top pan and set aside to cool.

5   To assemble cake, place a layer of meringue on a serving plate and spread with half the filling. Top with another meringue layer and remaining filling. Cut remaining meringue into squares and position at angles on top of cake. Drizzle with topping and decorate with cream.

ORANGE GATEAU

Serves 8
Oven temperature 350°F (180°C)

- ☐ 4 eggs
- ☐ ¹/₂ cup (120 mL) sugar
- ☐ ¹/₂ cup (120 mL) all-purpose flour, sifted
- ☐ ¹/₄ cup (60 mL) self-rising flour, sifted
- ☐ orange slices

ORANGE AND DATE FILLING
- ☐ 1 tablespoon brandy
- ☐ 1 tablespoon Cointreau
- ☐ 5 oz (155 g) fresh dates, pitted and chopped
- ☐ 3 tablespoons sugar
- ☐ ¹/₂ cup (120 mL) water
- ☐ 1 orange, peeled and chopped
- ☐ 1 egg, lightly beaten
- ☐ 3 tablespoons sugar
- ☐ 1¹/₂ tablespoons cornstarch
- ☐ ²/₃ cup (160 mL) milk, scalded
- ☐ 1 cup (140 mL) heavy cream

SUGAR PAPER
- ☐ ¹/₂ cup (120 mL) sugar
- ☐ ¹/₂ cup (120 mL) dark brown sugar
- ☐ 1 tablespoon coffee sugar crystals

ORANGE BUTTERCREAM TOPPING
- ☐ 3 egg yolks
- ☐ 3 tablespoons sugar
- ☐ ¹/₄ cup (60 mL) milk, scalded
- ☐ 2 drops orange food coloring
- ☐ 1 cup (240 mL) confectioners sugar
- ☐ 12 tablespoons unsalted butter, softened

1   Beat eggs and sugar in a mixing bowl, until mixture is thick and creamy and forms a ribbon. Fold through all-purpose and self-rising flours. Pour mixture into a greased and lined 8-inch (20 cm) cake pan and bake for 25-30 minutes, or until cooked through and golden. Stand in cake pan for 5 minutes before turning out onto a wire rack to cool.

2   To make filling, place brandy, Cointreau and dates in a bowl and set aside to stand for 30 minutes. Place sugar and water in a small saucepan and cook over a low heat, stirring constantly, until sugar dissolves. Add oranges, bring to the boil, then reduce heat and simmer for 20 minutes. Remove from heat and set aside to cool.

3   Drain oranges and add to date mixture. Combine egg, sugar and cornstarch in a saucepan, whisk in milk and cook over a low heat, stirring until mixture is smooth and thickens. Set aside to cool. Beat cream until soft peaks form. Fold through egg

mixture with dates and oranges.

4   To make Sugar Paper, sprinkle sugar, dark brown sugar and coffee sugar on an oven tray covered with greased foil. Place under a preheated hot broiler and cook until sugar caramelizes and melts into a thin sheet. Watch closely, as the sugar burns easily. Set aside to cool. Break into pieces.

5   To assemble gâteau, cut cake horizontally into three layers. Spread bottom layer with half the filling, top with second layer of cake, and spread with remaining filling. Top with remaining cake layer and refrigerate for 30 minutes.

6   To make buttercream, beat egg yolks and sugar until thick and creamy and mixture forms a ribbon. Whisk in scalded milk and pour mixture into the top of a double boiler and cook over simmering water until mixture thickens and coats the back of a wooden spoon. Stir in food coloring and set aside to cool. Place mixture in a mixing bowl and beat in confectioners sugar and butter a little at a time until mixture is creamy and stiff peaks form. Spread evenly over sides and top of cake. Decorate with Sugar Paper pieces and orange slices.

STEAMED PEAR PUDDING WITH CARAMEL SAUCE

Don't keep this pudding for a special occasion – it is just too good!

Serves 8

- ☐ **3 bosc pears, peeled, cored and finely chopped**
- ☐ **$^1/_2$ cup (120 mL) water**
- ☐ **1$^1/_2$ tablespoons sugar**
- ☐ **3 tablespoons butter**
- ☐ **3 tablespoons sugar**
- ☐ **2 eggs**
- ☐ **$^3/_4$ cup (180 mL) self-rising flour, sifted**
- ☐ **$^1/_4$ cup (60 mL) milk**

CARAMEL SAUCE
- ☐ **$^3/_4$ cup (180 mL) sugar**
- ☐ **3 tablespoons water**
- ☐ **3 tablespoons unsalted butter, cut into pieces**
- ☐ **$^2/_3$ cup (160 mL) heavy cream**

1   Place pears, water and sugar in a saucepan and cook over a medium heat for 10 minutes, or until pears are just tender. Remove from heat and set aside.

2   Cream butter and sugar until pale and fluffy. Add eggs and beat well. Sift flour over mixture and fold in with milk.

3   Strain pears and fold into pudding mixture. Pour into a greased 6 cup (1$^1/_2$ liter) capacity pudding basin. Cover with a round of lightly greased wax paper, then foil and pudding basin lid.

4   Place basin in a large saucepan with enough boiling water to come halfway up the side of the basin. Boil for 1$^1/_2$ hours, or until pudding is firm, replacing water if necessary as the pudding cooks. Allow to stand 5 minutes before turning out.

5   To make sauce, place sugar and water together in a heavy-based saucepan and cook over a medium heat, stirring until sugar dissolves. Cook until mixture caramelizes and is a deep amber color. Remove from heat. Add butter one piece at a time, stirring until melted. Return sauce to heat, pour in cream and cook, stirring, for 2 minutes. Remove from heat and set aside to cool. Serve with pudding.

Left: Chocolate Meringue Cake
Below: Steamed Pear Pudding with Caramel Sauce, Orange Gâteau

CHOCOHOLIC

The source of chocolate, the cacao tree, was one of the greatest discoveries made on the American continent. Chocolate's smooth, rich flavor is loved by almost everyone. Its scientific name is *Theobroma cacao* (*theobroma* means 'food of the gods').

Storing chocolate

Chocolate should be stored in a dry, airy place at a temperature of about 60°F (16°C). If stored in unsuitable conditions, the cocoa butter in chocolate may rise to the surface, leaving a white film. A similar discoloration occurs when water condenses on the surface. This often happens to refrigerated chocolates that are too loosely wrapped. Chocolate affected this way is still suitable for melting, however, it is unsuitable for grating.

Melting chocolate

Chocolate melts more rapidly if broken into small pieces. The melting process should occur slowly, as chocolate scorches if overheated. To melt chocolate, place it in the top of a double boiler and set aside. Fill the bottom part of pan with enough water to come just under top pan – the water should not touch the top pan. Bring water to the boil, then remove from heat and place chocolate over the hot water. Stand off the heat, stirring occasionally until chocolate melts and is of a smooth consistency. Remove top pan and cool at room temperature.

Watchpoints

❦ Do not melt chocolate over a direct flame.

❦ The container in which the chocolate is being melted should be kept uncovered and completely dry. Covering could cause condensation and just one drop of water will ruin the chocolate.

❦ Chocolate 'seizes' if it is over-heated, or if it comes into contact with water or steam. Seizing results in the chocolate tightening and becoming a thick mass that will not melt. To rescue seized chocolate, stir in a little cream or vegetable oil, until the chocolate becomes smooth again.

Compound chocolate

Compound chocolate, also called chocolate coating, is designed to replace couverture chocolate for coating. It can be purchased in block form or as round discs. Both forms are

available in milk or semi-sweet chocolate. Compound chocolate is made from a vegetable oil base with sugar, milk solids and flavoring. It contains cocoa powder, but not cocoa butter and is easy to melt. It does not require tempering and is the easiest form for beginners to work with.

Chocolate decorations

Chocolate caraques: Pour melted chocolate over a cool work surface such as marble, ceramic or granite. Spread the chocolate as smoothly as possible, using a flexible metal spatula, in a very thin layer. Do not leave any holes. If the chocolate is too thick it will not roll. Allow chocolate to set at room temperature. Holding a long sharp knife at a 45° angle, pull gently over the surface of the chocolate to form scrolls.

Chocolate curls and shavings: Chocolate curls are made from chocolate that is at room temperature. To make shavings, chill the chocolate first. Using a vegetable peeler, shave the sides of the chocolate. Curls or shavings will form depending on the temperature of the chocolate.

Chocolate leaves: Use stiff, fresh, non-poisonous leaves such as rose or lemon leaves. Keep as much stem as possible to hold onto. Wash and dry leaves, brush the shiny surface of the leaf with a thin layer of melted, cooled chocolate. Allow to set at room temperature then carefully peel away leaf.

Piping chocolate: Chocolate can be piped into fancy shapes for decorating desserts or cakes. Trace a simple design on a thin piece of paper. Tape a sheet of wax paper to the work surface and slide the drawing under the sheet of paper. Pipe over outline with melted chocolate. Set aside to firm at room temperature, then remove carefully with a metal spatula and use as desired.

Chocolates cases: Quarter fill mould with melted chocolate and tap to remove any air bubbles. Brush chocolate evenly up sides of mould to make a shell, then freeze for 2 minutes or until set. Larger chocolate cases to hold desserts can also be made in this way using foil-lined individual metal tart pans, brioche or muffin pans as moulds. When set, remove from pans and fill with a dessert filling such as mousse or a flavored cream.

China Mikassa

❧
CHOCOLATE
MOCHA CAKE

*A rich chocolate cake that could easily
become a favorite. Decorate with
chocolate leaves, curls or piped
decorations to make an extra-special
adult birthday cake.*

Serves 8
Oven temperature 320°F (160°C)

- ☐ **6¹/₂ oz (185 g) semi-sweet
  chocolate, broken into small
  pieces**
- ☐ **4 eggs, separated**
- ☐ **¹/₂ cup (120 mL) sugar**
- ☐ **12 tablespoons unsalted butter,
  softened and cut into pieces**
- ☐ **2 tablespoons strong black coffee**
- ☐ **¹/₂ cup (120 mL) all-purpose flour,
  sifted**

CHOCOLATE GLAZE
- ☐ **7 oz (200 g) semi-sweet
  chocolate, broken into small
  pieces**
- ☐ **7 tablespoons unsalted butter**
- ☐ **2 tablespoons water**

1   Place chocolate in top of a double
boiler and heat over simmering water for 5
minutes, or until chocolate melts. Remove
top pan from heat and stir until smooth.
Set aside to cool.
2   Place egg yolks and sugar in a bowl
and beat until pale and fluffy. Add butter
and beat mixture until creamy. Add coffee
and chocolate and continue beating
mixture until creamy. Sift flour over mixture
and fold in lightly.
3   Beat egg whites until soft peaks form.
Lightly fold egg white mixture into chocolate
mixture. Pour into a greased and lined 8-
inch (20 cm) cake pan and bake for 30
minutes, or until firm to touch. Turn off
oven and cool cake in oven with door ajar.
Remove from pan and refrigerate for 2
hours or overnight.
4   To make glaze, place chocolate, butter
and water in top of a double boiler and
heat over simmering water until chocolate
and butter melt. Remove top pan from
heat and stir ingredients to combine. Set
aside to cool.
5   Remove cake from refrigerator and
place on a wire rack. Place on a tray and
pour glaze over cake, smoothing it over
edges and onto sides with a spatula. Leave

until completely set. Transfer cake to a flat
serving platter and cut into slices to serve.

Variation
For chocoholics this cake can be made
even more special if you make two cakes,
then sandwich them together with
whipped cream and decorate the top with
chocolate caraques (see page 12).

Chocolate Mocha Cake

APPLE AND MASCARPONE STACKS

Serves 4
Oven temperature 350°F (180°C)

- [ ] **8 sheets filo pastry**
- [ ] **6 tablespoons butter, melted**
- [ ] **4 tablespoons sugar**
- [ ] **¹/₂ cup (120 mL) ground almonds**

APPLE FILLING
- [ ] **1 cup (240 mL) sugar**
- [ ] **¹/₂ cup (120 mL) water**
- [ ] **2 green apples, peeled, cored and thinly sliced**
- [ ] **3 tablespoons Calvados (apple brandy)**

MASCARPONE PRALINE FILLING
- [ ] **4 tablespoons sliced almonds, toasted**
- [ ] **2 tablespoons Calvados (apple brandy)**
- [ ] **18 oz (500 g) mascarpone; about 2¹/₂ cups (590 mL)**

TOFFEE SAUCE
- [ ] **²/₃ cup (160 mL) cream**
- [ ] **6 tablespoons butter**
- [ ] **³/₄ cup (180 mL) brown sugar**

1   Layer 4 sheets of pastry, brushing between each pastry layer with butter and sprinkling with a little sugar and almonds. Press layers together to seal, then cut into 3¹/₄-inch (8 cm) squares. Repeat with remaining pastry, butter, sugar and almonds. Place pastry squares onto greased cookie sheets and bake for 10-12 minutes, or until golden.

2   To make Apple Filling, place sugar and water in a saucepan and cook over a low heat, stirring until sugar dissolves. Add apples and Calvados, simmer until tender. Drain apples and reserve liquid.

3   To make Mascarpone Praline Filling, place reserved apple liquid in a clean pan and simmer until golden. Place almonds on a cookie sheet lined with aluminum foil, pour toffee over and set aside until toffee hardens. Break toffee into pieces, place in food processor and process to make coarse crumbs. Stir praline and Calvados into mascarpone.

4   To make sauce, combine cream, butter and brown sugar in a saucepan. Stir over a low heat until smooth. Set aside to keep warm.

5   To assemble stacks, place a pastry square on each serving plate, top with half the apple slices and half the Mascarpone Praline Filling. Repeat with remaining pastry squares and apple slices and filling, ending with a third layer of pastry. Top with toffee sauce and serve immediately.

Chocolate Fans, Berry and Rose Petal Tuiles, Apple and Mascarpone Stacks

---

EDIBLE FLOWERS

There are a number of flowers that are quite safe to eat and can be used to add color to desserts, salads and many other dishes. Some of the most common ones are roses, marigolds, zucchini, chrysanthemum, nasturtium and herb flowers such as borage, lavender and sage. But remember that some flowers are poisonous. If you are unsure always check before using them with food.

CHOCOLATE FANS

Serves 4

CHOCOLATE ROUNDS
- [ ] **4¹/₂ oz (125 g) white chocolate, melted**
- [ ] **4¹/₂ oz (125 g) milk chocolate, melted**
- [ ] **9 oz (250 g) semi-sweet chocolate, melted**

MOCHA CREAM
- [ ] **6¹/₂ oz (185 g) semi-sweet chocolate**
- [ ] **4 tablespoons heavy cream**
- [ ] **3 tablespoons Tia Maria**
- [ ] **2 tablespoons butter**

PRALINE CREAM
- [ ] **¹/₂ cup (120 mL) sugar**

☐ **3 tablespoons water**
☐ **3 tablespoons blanched almonds, toasted**
☐ **$^2/_3$ cup (160 mL) heavy cream, whipped**

1   To make Chocolate Rounds, line four cookie sheets with wax paper. Spread white chocolate on one tray and milk chocolate on another. Spread half the semi-sweet chocolate on each of the remaining cookie sheets. Spread out chocolate, using a spatula, to form 9$^1/_2$ x 6$^1/_2$-inch (24 x 16 cm) rectangles. Set aside to firm at room temperature. Cut four 3$^1/_4$-inch (8 cm) circles from each rectangle of chocolate, using a pastry cutter.

2   To make Mocha Cream, place chocolate, cream, Tia Maria and butter in a saucepan and cook over a low heat until

mixture is smooth. Remove from heat and cool for 5 minutes then beat until creamy.

3   To make Praline Cream, place sugar and water in a small saucepan, cook over a low heat, stirring until sugar dissolves. Increase heat and simmer sugar syrup until golden. Place almonds on a cookie sheet, pour caramel over and set aside until caramel hardens. Break almond brittle into pieces and place in a food processor and process to make small crumbs. Fold praline through whipped cream.

4   To assemble fans, place a semi-sweet chocolate round on each serving plate. Using half the Mocha Cream spread each round with it, then top with a milk chocolate round and spread with Praline Cream. Top with a white chocolate round and spread with remaining Mocha Cream.

Finally top with remaining semi-sweet chocolate rounds and press each stack gently on the back to fan out.

BERRY AND ROSE PETAL TUILES

These thin French cookies shaped into baskets and filled with fresh berries make a sophisticated and elegant dessert for a special occasion.

Serves 6
Oven temperature 350°F (180°C)

TUILES
☐ **3 tablespoons all-purpose flour**
☐ **4 tablespoons butter, melted**
☐ **3 tablespoons sugar**
☐ **3 tablespoons ground almonds**
☐ **2 egg whites**
☐ **2 teaspoons rosewater**

BERRY FILLING
☐ **1$^1/_2$ pints mixed berries, such as strawberries, raspberries, blackberries and boysenberries**
☐ **3 miniature roses, petals removed**

ROSE CREAM
☐ **1 teaspoon rosewater**
☐ **pink food coloring**
☐ **$^2/_3$ cup (160 mL) heavy cream, whipped**

1   To make tuiles, combine flour, butter, sugar, ground almonds, egg whites and rosewater in a bowl and refrigerate for 20 minutes. Trim white base from rose petals, wash and pat dry.

2   Mark two 4$^3/_4$-inch (12 cm) circles on a greased and floured cookie sheet. Place a tablespoon of tuile mixture in each circle and spread out thinly to fill circles. Bake for 10-12 minutes.

3   Remove cookie sheet from oven and carefully lift cookies from cookie sheet using a spatula. Press cookies over base of a greased, small, flat-bottomed bowl to form a basket. Set aside to cool. Repeat with tuile mixture to make six baskets.

4   Fill cooled baskets with mixed berries and rose petals.

5   To make cream, fold rosewater and a few drops of food coloring through cream. Serve with filled tuiles.

FOOD WITH SPIRIT

A dash of liqueur, or a splash of champagne, add that special touch to a dish. These recipes use a little alcohol to add that feeling of indulgence. Remember when using alcohol in cooking that more does not necessarily mean better.

LOBSTER PASTRIES WITH CHAMPAGNE SAUCE

Fresh asparagus, lobster and champagne – the ultimate indulgence.

Serves 6
Oven temperature 400°F (200°C)

- ☐ **6 oz (175 g) prepared or ready-rolled puff pastry, thawed**
- ☐ **1 tablespoon water**
- ☐ **2 tablespoons sliced almonds**

CHAMPAGNE SAUCE
- ☐ **1 cup (240 mL) chicken stock**
- ☐ **$^1/_2$ cup (120 mL) champagne**
- ☐ **2 teaspoons grated lemon zest**
- ☐ **1 cup (240 mL) heavy cream**
- ☐ **1 egg yolk, lightly beaten**
- ☐ **2 tablespoons butter mixed with 2 tablespoons all-purpose flour**
- ☐ **1 teaspoon finely chopped fresh coriander**
- ☐ **freshly ground black pepper**

FILLING
- ☐ **9 oz (250 g) fresh asparagus, trimmed and cut into 3-inch (7 cm) lengths**
- ☐ **2 uncooked lobster tails**
- ☐ **3 sprigs fresh coriander**
- ☐ **bouquet garni**
- ☐ **1 teaspoon whole green peppercorns**
- ☐ **$^1/_2$ bunch watercress**

1   Cut pastry into six 4 x 2-inch (10 x 5 cm) rectangles and place on a greased cookie sheet. Brush lightly with water and sprinkle with almonds. Bake for 15 minutes, reduce oven temperature to 350°F (180°C) and cook for 10 minutes longer, or until pastry is golden brown and crisp. Set aside to cool on wire rack. Cut each rectangle into three horizontal layers.

2   To make Champagne Sauce, place stock, champagne and lemon rind in a small saucepan. Bring to the boil and boil until liquid is reduced by half. Strain and return to a clean pan. Combine cream and egg yolk and whisk into liquid. Whisk in butter mixture and cook over a low heat, without boiling, stirring constantly, until sauce thickens slightly. Stir coriander through sauce and season to taste with black pepper. Set aside and keep warm.

3   To make filling, boil, steam or microwave asparagus until tender. Refresh under cold running water. Drain and set aside. Place lobster tails, coriander, bouquet garni and peppercorns in a saucepan. Cover with water and simmer for 10-15 minutes or until cooked. Remove lobster tails from water and set aside to cool for 10 minutes. Shell tails and cut into thin medallions.

4   To serve, warm pastry rectangles in a low oven for 5 minutes. Place bottom layers on six serving plates. Top with half the asparagus and half the lobster and a few sprigs of watercress. Spoon sauce over. Repeat with remaining pastry, asparagus, lobster, watercress and sauce, finishing with almond pastry layer.

Lobster Pastries with Champagne Sauce

radicchio, watercress and pear in a serving bowl. Top with quail, sprinkle with pecans and drizzle sauce over. Serve immediately.

LOIN OF LAMB WITH PORT SAUCE

Loin of lamb, leeks and a port sauce make up this easy-to-prepare dish. Served with new potatoes and a salad of mixed lettuces and fresh herbs, you have a wonderfully indulgent meal.

Serves 6

- [ ] **3 tablespoons sugar**
- [ ] **3 tablespoons red wine vinegar**
- [ ] **1$^1/_2$ cups (355 mL) beef stock**
- [ ] **10 tablespoons butter**
- [ ] **6 leeks, cut into $^1/_2$-inch (1 cm) slices**
- [ ] **3 tablespoons water**
- [ ] **2 tablespoons oil**
- [ ] **3 boneless loins of lamb, trimmed of all visible fat and skin removed**
- [ ] **4 tablespoons port**
- [ ] **freshly ground black pepper**

1   Place sugar and vinegar in a small saucepan and cook over a low heat until sugar dissolves. Bring to the boil and boil until mixture caramelizes. Stir in stock and simmer for 10 minutes. Set aside.

2   Melt 7 tablespoons butter in a heavy-based skillet, add leek slices and water and cook gently for 8 minutes, or until leeks are just tender. Set aside and keep warm.

3   Heat remaining butter and oil in a large heavy-based skillet. When sizzling, add loins of lamb and cook for 5-7 minutes each side, or until browned. Remove from skillet and set aside to keep warm. Place skillet over a medium heat, add port and cook, scraping up caramelized juices in skillet. Stir in reserved stock mixture and cook over a medium heat until sauce reduces and thickens. Season to taste with black pepper.

4   Divide leeks between six serving plates. Slice each loin of lamb into medallions and arrange on top of leeks. Spoon sauce over and serve immediately.

China Wedgwood *Silverware* Oneida

MARSALA QUAIL SALAD

In this salad the quail and marsala, with their distinctive flavors, mingle deliciously with the salad leaves. An elegant dish that can be served as a luncheon dish or starter.

Serves 6
Oven temperature 350°F (180°C)

- [ ] **6 quail**
- [ ] **2 tablespoons butter**
- [ ] **$^1/_2$ cup (120 mL) heavy cream**
- [ ] **$^3/_4$ cup (180 mL) dry Marsala**
- [ ] **1 head curly endive, leaves separated**
- [ ] **1 Belgian endive, leaves separated**
- [ ] **1 radicchio, leaves separated**
- [ ] **1 bunch watercress**
- [ ] **1 pear, peeled, cored and sliced**
- [ ] **$^1/_3$ cup pecans**

MARSALA SAUCE
- [ ] **$^1/_2$ cup (120 mL) heavy cream**
- [ ] **2 tablespoons mayonnaise**
- [ ] **2 teaspoons dry Marsala**

1   Place quail on a rack in a baking pan and bake for 20 minutes. Cool slightly, then break into serving-size portions.

2   Melt butter in a saucepan. Add cream and Marsala, bring to the boil, then reduce heat and simmer for 5 minutes. Add quail and cook for 5 minutes longer. Set aside to cool.

3   To make sauce, combine cream, mayonnaise and Marsala and beat well to combine.

4   Arrange curly endive, Belgian endive,

FIG AND APPLE SOUFFLE

This light-as-air soufflé, fragrant with brandy and figs, is a delicious way to end any meal.

Serves 8
Oven temperature 350°F (180°C)

- ☐ **5$^1/_2$ oz (155 g) dried figs, finely chopped**
- ☐ **2 tablespoons Calvados (apple brandy)**
- ☐ **$^1/_2$ cup (120 mL) apple sauce**
- ☐ **3 tablespoons sugar**
- ☐ **4 egg whites**

1   Place figs and Calvados in a bowl and toss to combine. Set aside to macerate for 2 hours.
2   Combine apple sauce, sugar, and fig mixture in a mixing bowl and stir until sugar dissolves.
3   Lightly grease a 1 quart (1 liter) soufflé dish and sprinkle with a little sugar. Beat egg whites until stiff peaks form. Fold egg whites into apple mixture and spoon into prepared soufflé dish. Stand soufflé dish in a baking pan and pour in enough boiling water to come halfway up sides of dish. Bake for 20-25 minutes, or until well risen and firm to touch.

DID YOU KNOW?

❦   Figs are one of the ancient fruits originally from the Middle East and Mediterranean areas.
❦   The people of the Mediterranean consider the fig to be so important that they have made it a symbol of peace and plenty.
❦   Figs are a member of the mulberry family and there are over 700 varieties.
❦   Fresh figs should be served at room temperature when their wonderful sweet flavor is at its best.

Fig and Apple Souffle

China Villeroy & Boch

BEEF WRAPPED IN PASTRY WITH RED WINE SAUCE

Succulent beef surrounded by mushrooms and wrapped in puff pastry, this dish is sure to impress – this Master Class shows you how easy it is.

Serves 6
Oven temperature 425°F (220°C)

- [ ] **4 tablespoons butter**
- [ ] **2¹/₄ pounds (1 kg) beef tenderloin, in one piece, trimmed**
- [ ] **1 onion, chopped**
- [ ] **13 oz (375 g) small white mushrooms, finely chopped**
- [ ] **freshly ground black pepper**
- [ ] **pinch ground nutmeg**
- [ ] **1 tablespoon finely chopped fresh parsley**
- [ ] **18 oz (500 g) prepared or ready-rolled puff pastry, thawed**
- [ ] **1 egg, lightly beaten**

RED WINE SAUCE
- [ ] **1 cup (240 mL) red wine**
- [ ] **1 teaspoon finely chopped fresh thyme, or ¹/₄ teaspoon dried thyme**
- [ ] **1 teaspoon finely chopped fresh parsley**
- [ ] **freshly ground black pepper**
- [ ] **7 tablespoons butter, cut into eight pieces**
- [ ] **2 teaspoons cornstarch, blended with 1 tablespoon water**

1   Melt half the butter in a heavy-based skillet. When sizzling, add beef and cook over a medium heat for 10 minutes, turning to brown and seal on all sides. Remove skillet from heat and set aside to cool completely.

2   Melt remaining butter in skillet and cook onion for 5 minutes, or until soft. Add mushrooms and cook over a medium heat for 15 minutes, or until mushrooms give up all their juices, and these evaporate. Stir during cooking to prevent them sticking. Season to taste with black pepper and nutmeg, stir in parsley and set aside to cool completely.

3   Roll out pastry to a length 3¹/₄ inches (8 cm) longer than meat and wide enough to wrap around it. Spread half mushroom mixture down centre of pastry and place meat on top. Spread remaining mushroom mixture on top of meat. Cut corners out of pastry. Brush pastry edges with egg. Wrap pastry around meat like a parcel, tucking ends in. Turn pastry-wrapped beef over and place on a lightly greased cookie sheet and freeze for 10 minutes.

4   Roll out remaining pastry to a 12 x 4-inches (30 x 10 cm) length and cut into strips ¹/₂-inch (1 cm) wide. Remove beef from freezer and brush pastry all over with egg. Arrange 5 pastry strips diagonally over pastry parcel, then arrange remaining strips diagonally in opposite direction. Brush top of strips only with egg. Bake for 30 minutes for medium-rare beef. Place on a warmed serving platter and set aside to rest in a warm place for 10 minutes.

5   To make sauce, place wine in a small saucepan and cook over a medium heat until reduced by half. Add thyme and parsley and season to taste with black pepper. Remove pan from heat and quickly whisk in 1 piece of butter at a time, ensuring that each piece of butter is completely whisked in and melted before adding next. Pour in cornstarch mixture and stir over a medium heat until sauce thickens. Serve with sliced beef.

Roll out pastry to a length 3¹/₄ inches (8 cm) longer than meat and wide enough to wrap around it. Spread half mushroom mixture down centre of pastry, and remaining mixture on top of meat.

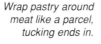

Wrap pastry around meat like a parcel, tucking ends in.

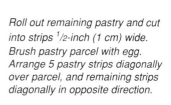

Roll out remaining pastry and cut into strips ¹/₂-inch (1 cm) wide. Brush pastry parcel with egg. Arrange 5 pastry strips diagonally over parcel, and remaining strips diagonally in opposite direction.

Props Accoutrement

OYSTER MOUSSELINE WITH CHAMPAGNE SAUCE

Just right as a starter for a summer dinner party. These delicious mousselines have a subtle flavor and are perfectly complemented by the accompanying Champagne Sauce.

Serves 6
Oven temperature 350°F (180°C)

- ☐ **36 oysters**
- ☐ **2 oz (60 g) scallops**
- ☐ **2 oz (60 g) John Dory fillets, skinned**
- ☐ **2 egg whites**
- ☐ **1 egg yolk**
- ☐ **$^1/_4$ cup (60 mL) heavy cream**
- ☐ **freshly ground black pepper**
- ☐ **12 Boston lettuce leaves, blanched**

CHAMPAGNE SAUCE
- ☐ **$^1/_2$ cup (120 mL) champagne**
- ☐ **$^1/_4$ cup (60 mL) heavy cream**
- ☐ **14 tablespoons unsalted butter, cut into pieces**

1   Place oysters, scallops and John Dory in a food processor or blender and process until smooth. Press through a sieve. Place oyster mixture in a stainless steel bowl over ice. Beat egg whites until soft peaks form and set aside. Whisk egg yolk into cream a little at a time, then lightly fold in egg whites. Season to taste with black pepper.
2   Line six lightly greased, individual ramekins with lettuce leaves, allowing leaves to overhang top. Divide fish mixture evenly between ramekins and fold leaves over.
3   Cover each ramekin with foil. Place ramekins in a baking dish and pour in enough hot water to come halfway up sides of ramekins. Bake for 35-40 minutes, or until a skewer inserted in the centre comes out clean. Set aside for 5 minutes before turning out.
4   To make sauce, place champagne in a saucepan, bring to the boil and cook until reduced by half. Stir in cream and simmer until sauce is reduced and of a creamy consistency. Gradually whisk in butter a piece at a time. Whisk well after each addition. Serve with mousseline.

Marinated Pork Spare Ribs, Oyster Mousseline with Champagne Sauce, Orange Liqueur Babas

ORANGE LIQUEUR BABAS

An adaptation of the traditional rum baba, this recipe uses Grand Marnier in place of rum. It is said that the original rum baba came about when the Polish king Stanislas Leszcsunski was exiled to Lorraine. He found the kugelhopf too dry and so poured rum over it, then named it after his favorite hero, Ali Baba.

Serves 4
Oven temperature 400°F (200°C)

- ☐ **1 cup (240 mL) all-purpose flour, sifted**
- ☐ **1$^1/_2$ teaspoons dried yeast**
- ☐ **1 teaspoon sugar**
- ☐ **5 tablespoons butter, melted**
- ☐ **2 eggs, lightly beaten**
- ☐ **$^1/_4$ cup (60 mL) milk, warmed**
- ☐ **2 tablespoons finely chopped candied pineapple**
- ☐ **2 tablespoons finely chopped candied apricots**

ORANGE SYRUP
- ☐ **$^1/_2$ cup (120 mL) water**
- ☐ **3 tablespoons sugar**
- ☐ **2 tablespoons orange juice**
- ☐ **2 tablespoons Grand Marnier**

APRICOT GLAZE
- ☐ **2 tablespoons strained apricot jam, warmed with 1$^1/_2$ tablespoons water**
- ☐ **crystalized orange rind**

1   Combine flour, yeast and sugar in a mixing bowl. Whisk butter, eggs and milk together and beat into flour mixture. Continue to beat for 3-4 minutes.
2   Stir pineapple and apricots into batter. Spoon batter into six, greased individual baba moulds – the mixture should only one-third fill the moulds. Cover each mould with plastic wrap and set aside in a warm place to rise for 30 minutes, or until mixture doubles in size. Uncover, bake for 15-20 minutes, or until golden and cooked through. Remove from oven and set aside to cool in moulds.
3   To make Orange Syrup, place water and sugar in a small saucepan and cook over a low heat, stirring constantly, until sugar dissolves. Bring to the boil and simmer for 5 minutes, without stirring. Remove from heat and stir in orange juice and Grand Marnier. Prick cooled babas with a skewer and pour hot syrup over. Set aside to cool.
4   Turn babas out and brush with apricot glaze. Decorate with crystalized orange rind.

MARINATED PORK SPARE RIBS

American pork spare ribs are a barbecue favorite. In this recipe they are marinated in wine with rosemary and fennel seeds and glazed with wine and mustard to make an extra-special dish.

Serves 4
Oven temperature 400°F (200°C)

- ☐ **4 racks pork spare ribs, each with 6 ribs**
- ☐ **2 tablespoons vegetable oil**

MARINADE
- ☐ **1$^1/_2$ tablespoons coarse salt**
- ☐ **$^1/_2$ cup (120 mL) sugar**
- ☐ **6 sprigs fresh rosemary, chopped**
- ☐ **3 tablespoons fennel seeds**
- ☐ **coarsely grated zest 2 oranges**
- ☐ **1 cup (240 mL) white wine**

WINE AND MUSTARD SAUCE
- ☐ **3 tablespoons white wine**
- ☐ **2 tablespoons wholegrain mustard**
- ☐ **2 tablespoons red currant jelly**

1   To make marinade, combine coarse salt, sugar, rosemary, fennel seeds, orange rind and wine in a large flat dish. Cut ribs into groups of two. Add ribs and turn to coat well, cover and refrigerate overnight. Turn occasionally.
2   Heat oil in a large roasting pan. Remove ribs from marinade and place in roasting pan, bake for 15-20 minutes, basting occasionally with marinade. Remove ribs from pan and set aside to keep warm.
3   To make sauce, pour excess oil from pan, place pan over a high heat, add wine and cook, scraping up caramelised juices in pan. Stir in mustard and jelly and mix well to combine. Continue to cook until sauce is thick and syrupy. Just prior to serving, return ribs to pan and toss in sauce to coat.

SUPER SAUCES

Hollandaise Sauce turns salmon into a really special treat. Fresh homemade pesto makes pasta a luxury and velouté is the base for many of the best sauces. With this selection of sauces you can add that special touch to a meal in next to no time.

From top: Pesto Sauce, Indulgent Mayonnaise, Creamy Broccoli Sauce, Hollandaise Sauce, Rich Tomato Sauce, White Wine Vinaigrette

CREAMY BROCCOLI SAUCE

Serve this sauce as soon as it is made. It is delicious tossed through cooked pasta or served with chicken or fish.

Makes 3 cups (700 mL)

- [ ] **1 head broccoli, broken into small florets**
- [ ] **2 tablespoons butter**
- [ ] **2 teaspoons wholegrain mustard**
- [ ] **6 green onions, finely chopped**
- [ ] **3 tablespoons all-purpose flour**
- [ ] **$1^3/_4$ cups (410 mL) chicken stock**
- [ ] **3 tablespoons white wine**
- [ ] **$^1/_2$ cup (120 mL) heavy cream**
- [ ] **$1^1/_2$ teaspoons grated lemon rind**
- [ ] **freshly ground black pepper**

1   Boil, steam or microwave broccoli until tender. Drain and refresh under cold running water. Drain and set aside.
2   Melt butter in a saucepan, then add mustard and green onions and cook over a medium heat for 2-3 minutes. Stir in flour and cook for 1 minute longer. Gradually stir in stock and wine and cook, stirring constantly, until sauce boils and thickens.
3   Remove pan from heat and blend in cream, lemon rind, and black pepper to taste. Place broccoli in a food processor or blender and process until smooth. Stir broccoli into sauce and heat gently.

RICH TOMATO SAUCE

Serve this sauce with any boiled, steamed or microwaved vegetables. Top with breadcrumbs and Parmesan cheese and place under a hot broiler to create a tomato-flavored gratin.

Makes 2 cups (480 mL)

- [ ] **2 tablespoons olive oil**
- [ ] **2 leeks, white part finely sliced**
- [ ] **1 can (16 oz/450 g) tomato purée**
- [ ] **2 cans (16 oz/450 g each) plum tomatoes, finely chopped and with their juice**
- [ ] **3 tablespoons tomato paste**
- [ ] **2 teaspoons finely chopped fresh rosemary**
- [ ] **1 tablespoon finely chopped fresh basil**
- [ ] **2 cloves garlic, crushed**
- [ ] **1 cup (240 mL) canned beef broth**
- [ ] **$^1/_2$ teaspoon sugar**
- [ ] **freshly ground black pepper**

1   Heat oil in a heavy saucepan and cook leeks over a medium heat for 4-5 minutes, or until soft.
2   Stir in tomato purée, tomatoes, tomato paste, rosemary, basil, garlic, beef broth, sugar, and black pepper to taste. Cook over a low heat, stirring frequently, for 1 hour or until sauce thickens.

WHITE WINE VINAIGRETTE

It is easy to alter the flavour of this vinaigrette by using different oils and different vinegars. You might like to try walnut or hazelnut oil, or a red wine or cider vinegar.

Makes 1 cup (240 mL)

- [ ] **4 tablespoons olive oil**
- [ ] **4 tablespoons peanut oil**
- [ ] **3 tablespoons white wine vinegar**
- [ ] **1 tablespoon Dijon mustard**
- [ ] **freshly ground black pepper**

Place olive oil, peanut oil, vinegar, mustard and black pepper to taste in a screwtop jar. Shake well to combine all ingredients.

Variations

Lemon Herb Vinaigrette: Replace vinegar with 3 tablespoons lemon juice, and add $^1/_2$ cup (120 mL) mixed chopped fresh herbs. Suggested herbs include basil, parsley, chives, rosemary, thyme or tarragon.
Hazelnut Vinaigrette: Replace olive oil with 4 tablespoons hazelnut oil and peanut oil with 4 tablespoons polyunsaturated oil. You might also like to add some finely chopped hazelnuts to the dressing just before serving.

VELOUTE

The base of the Creamy Broccoli Sauce is a velouté sauce. This sauce forms the base of many of the best sauces.

❧ A velouté sauce is a white sauce that uses milk or stock, or a combination of the two, as the liquid.
❧ The flavor and colour can be changed by using different vegetable purées and stocks.
❧ Omitting the vegetable purée and mustard gives a true velouté sauce that will stand on its own as an accompaniment to eggs, fish, poultry veal and vegetables.
❧ When making the sauce to go with fish use fish stock.

Right: Rich Tomato Sauce
Above: Pesto Sauce

❦
INDULGENT MAYONNAISE

Thick, creamy homemade mayonnaise is easy to make using a food processor and adds a touch of indulgence to any salad.

Makes 2 cups (480 mL)

- ☐ **6 egg yolks**
- ☐ **1 teaspoon Dijon mustard**
- ☐ **1 tablespoon lime juice**
- ☐ **1 tablespoon tarragon vinegar**
- ☐ **1 cup (240 mL) grapeseed oil**
- ☐ **1 cup (240 mL) peanut oil**
- ☐ **freshly ground black pepper**
- ☐ **1 tablespoon boiling water**

1　Place egg yolks, mustard, lime juice and vinegar in a food processor or blender and process until well mixed. Combine grapeseed oil and peanut oil. With machine running, slowly pour in oil mixture and process until mixture thickens.
2　Season to taste with black pepper and stir in water. Transfer to a jar, cover and refrigerate until required.

Variations

Garlic Mayonnaise: Add 6 cloves peeled garlic to the egg yolk mixture and replace lime juice and tarragon vinegar with 2 tablespoons lemon juice.

Green Herbed Mayonnaise: Replace lime juice and tarragon vinegar with 2 tablespoons cider vinegar. Purée ¹/₂ cup (120 mL) fresh basil leaves, 2 tablespoons fresh parsley, 12 fresh chives and 1 clove garlic. Blend into prepared mayonnaise.

❦
PESTO SAUCE

This traditional Italian sauce with its garlic and basil flavor is marvellous to have on hand to pep up vegetable soups, sauces, or just to toss through hot vegetables or pasta. Pesto can be stored in the refrigerator for up to two weeks.

Makes 1¹/₄ cup (300 mL)

- ☐ **1 cup (240 mL) fresh basil leaves**
- ☐ **4 cloves garlic, crushed**
- ☐ **4 tablespoons pine nuts, toasted**
- ☐ **¹/₂ cup (120 mL) grated fresh Parmesan cheese**
- ☐ **²/₃ cup (160 mL) olive oil**

Place basil, garlic and pine nuts in a food processor or blender and process until combined. Add cheese and oil and process until smooth.

❦
HOLLANDAISE SAUCE

The secret to success when making this sauce is to have the temperature right; it should be hot enough to thicken the sauce but not so hot that it will curdle. To achieve this, set the bowl over simmering water during cooking.

Makes 1 cup (240 mL)

- ☐ **3¹/₂ tablespoons white vinegar**
- ☐ **1¹/₂ tablespoons water**
- ☐ **12 whole peppercorns**
- ☐ **1 bay leaf**
- ☐ **3 egg yolks**
- ☐ **14 tablespoons butter, softened**
- ☐ **freshly ground black pepper**

1　Place vinegar, water, peppercorns and bay leaf in a saucepan. Bring to the boil and boil until mixture reduces to a third. Remove from heat and set aside to cool.
2　Place egg yolks in a heatproof bowl and whisk with 2 tablespoons butter. Strain vinegar mixture and whisk into egg mixture. Place bowl over a saucepan of simmering water and whisk constantly until mixture thickens.
3　Remove saucepan from heat and whisk in remaining butter, a little at a time, until sauce is thick, shiny and resembles a thick cream. Season to taste with black pepper and serve immediately.

Variation

Bearnaise Sauce: Add 3 finely chopped green onions to vinegar mixture, replace white vinegar with tarragon vinegar and make in the same way as for Hollandaise Sauce.

SEAFOOD SPECTACULAR

As a light main course or appetizer for a dinner party, seafood is a popular indulgence. These recipes use easy techniques to retain the wonderful flavors, but have an added twist to place them in the realm of super indulgences.

SALAD OF LOBSTER WITH RASPBERRIES

Lobster would have to be the undisputed king of shellfish. In this recipe, it is taken to new heights with the addition of a raspberry dressing.

Serves 4

- ☐ **2 lobster tails, cooked and shells removed**
- ☐ **1 small head radicchio, leaves separated**
- ☐ **1 small Boston lettuce, leaves separated**
- ☐ **1 small bunch watercress**
- ☐ **1 orange, segmented**
- ☐ **$1/2$ pint (240 mL) strawberries, halved**

DRESSING
- ☐ **$1/2$ cup (120 mL) fresh or frozen raspberries**
- ☐ **2 tablespoons raspberry vinegar**
- ☐ **2 tablespoons vegetable oil**
- ☐ **1 teaspoon finely chopped fresh mint**
- ☐ **1 tablespoon sugar**

1 Cut lobster tails into $1/2$-inch (1 cm) medallions and set aside.

2 Arrange radicchio, Boston lettuce, watercress, lobster, orange segments and strawberries attractively on a serving platter and refrigerate until required.

3 To make dressing, place raspberries in a food processor or blender and process until puréed. Press through a sieve to remove seeds. Combine raspberry purée with vinegar, oil, mint and sugar. Mix well to combine, pour over salad and serve immediately.

Salad of Lobster with Raspberries

China Noritake *Glass & Bowl* Bohemia Crystal

MUSSEL AND VEGETABLE TARTS

Serves 4
Oven temperature 425°F (220°C)

PASTRY
- ☐ 1¹/₂ cups (355 mL) all-purpose flour
- ☐ ¹/₄ teaspoon baking powder
- ☐ 8 tablespoons butter, cubed and chilled
- ☐ 1 egg yolk
- ☐ 1-2 tablespoons iced water
- ☐ ¹/₂ teaspoon lemon juice

FILLING
- ☐ 16 mussels, scrubbed and de-bearded
- ☐ 1 leek, cut into thin strips
- ☐ 2 large carrots, cut into thin julienne strips
- ☐ 1 tablespoon finely chopped fresh coriander
- ☐ 1¹/₄ cups (300 mL) heavy cream
- ☐ 12 jumbo shrimp, peeled and deveined

China Incorporated Agencies

LIME BATTERED SEAFOOD WITH MAYONNAISE

Never before have fish and french fries been this good. Make your own fries and no one will be able to resist.

Serves 4

- ☐ 8 jumbo shrimp, peeled, tails attached and deveined
- ☐ 2 squid, cleaned and cut into rings
- ☐ 4 thick white fish fillets, such as whiting or bream
- ☐ oil for cooking

BATTER
- ☐ 1¹/₂ cups (355 mL) all-purpose flour
- ☐ ¹/₂ cup (120 mL) lime juice
- ☐ 1 cup (240 mL) club soda
- ☐ 2 teaspoons finely grated lime zest

MAYONNAISE
- ☐ 3 egg yolks
- ☐ ¹/₄ teaspoon dry mustard
- ☐ 1 cup (240 mL) vegetable oil
- ☐ 2 tablespoons lemon juice
- ☐ 1 tablespoon finely chopped fresh coriander
- ☐ freshly ground black pepper

1   To make batter, place flour in a bowl and gradually stir in lime juice and club soda. Mix well to combine, then stir in lime zest. Set aside.

2   To make mayonnaise, place egg yolks and mustard in a food processor or blender and, with machine running, slowly pour in oil and process until mixture thickens. Blend in lemon juice. Stir in coriander and season to taste with black pepper.

3   Heat oil in a large saucepan. Dip shrimp, squid and fish in batter, drain off excess and cook a few at a time in hot oil, until golden. Remove from pan and drain on paper towels. Serve with mayonnaise.

Above: Lime Battered Seafood with Mayonnaise
Right: Mussel and Vegetable Tarts, Mixed Seafood with Parsley Cream

- □ **1¹/₂ tablespoons all-purpose flour**
- □ **2 tablespoons butter, softened**
- □ **freshly ground black pepper**

1   To make pastry, place flour, baking powder and butter in a food processor or blender and process until mixture resembles coarse breadcrumbs. Combine egg yolk, water and lemon juice and, with machine running, gradually pour in egg mixture, until a soft dough forms. Wrap in plastic wrap. Refrigerate for 1 hour.

2   Divide pastry into four portions and roll out thinly on a lightly floured surface. Line four 4-5-inch (10-12.5 cm) tart pans with pastry, prick base of tarts with a fork. Line tarts with parchment paper and fill with uncooked rice. Bake for 5 minutes, remove paper and rice, bake for 12 minutes longer.

3   To make filling, place mussels in a large saucepan and add just enough water to cover mussels. Cook over a low heat until shells open. Discard unopened shells. Remove mussel meat and discard shells. Reserve ¹/₂ cup (120 mL) of pan liquid. Heat reserved liquid in a skillet and cook leek, carrot and coriander for 2 minutes.

4   Stir in cream, mussels and shrimp and cook over a low heat for 5 minutes. Mix flour and butter together to form a paste, then whisk into cream mixture and cook for 2-3 minutes, or until thickened. Season to taste with black pepper. Spoon filling into warm pastry shells and serve.

❧

MIXED SEAFOOD WITH PARSLEY CREAM

Serves 4

- □ **5 tablespoons olive oil**
- □ **3 cloves garlic, crushed**
- □ **3¹/₂ oz (100 g) snapper or sea bass fillets, cut into 8 pieces**
- □ **3¹/₂ oz (100 g) ocean trout fillets, skinned and cut into 8 pieces**
- □ **8 jumbo shrimp, peeled and deveined**
- □ **8 scallops**
- □ **4 scampi (or langoustines), meat removed from tail**

TOMATO SALAD
- □ **3 ripe tomatoes, peeled, seeded and diced**
- □ **1¹/₂ tablespoons chopped fresh coriander**
- □ **1 tablespoon olive oil**
- □ **freshly ground black pepper**

PARSLEY CREAM
- □ **5 tablespoons finely chopped fresh parsley**
- □ **3 tablespoons heavy cream**
- □ **3 tablespoons mayonnaise**

1   To make salad, place tomatoes, coriander, oil, and black pepper to taste in a bowl and toss to combine. Set aside.

2   To make cream, place parsley, cream and mayonnaise in a food processor or blender and process until smooth.

3   Heat oil in a skillet and cook garlic, snapper, ocean trout, shrimp, scallops and scampi over a low heat for 6-7 minutes. Turn seafood gently during cooking, taking care not to damage whole pieces. Arrange seafood and salad on serving plates, drizzle Parsley Cream over and serve.

China Incorporated Agencies Silverware R.P. Symons

❧
SALMON AND PERCH MOSAIC WITH SORREL SAUCE

Your guests will be hooked on this luxurious combination of salmon, perch and spinach that is perfectly complemented by a creamy sauce.

Serves 4

- [ ] **4 large white fish fillets, such as perch**
- [ ] **2 tablespoons lemon juice**
- [ ] **freshly ground white pepper**
- [ ] **16 large spinach leaves, stalks removed and blanched**
- [ ] **2 salmon fillets, skinned**
- [ ] **4 square pieces aluminum foil, buttered**

SAUCE
- [ ] **3 tablespoons unsalted butter**
- [ ] **2 tablespoons chopped scallions**
- [ ] **1 clove garlic, chopped**
- [ ] **2 fresh sage leaves**
- [ ] **2$^{1}/_{2}$ cups (600 mL) young sorrel leaves**
- [ ] **2 cups (480 mL) fish stock**
- [ ] **1 bay leaf**
- [ ] **$^{1}/_{2}$ cup (120 mL) dry white wine**
- [ ] **1 cup (240 mL) heavy cream**
- [ ] **freshly ground black pepper**

1   Cut each fish fillet into four strips lengthways, each measuring 6 x 1-inch (15 x 2 cm) (this will give you sixteen strips). Sprinkle with 1 tablespoon lemon juice and season to taste with white pepper. Wrap each strip in blanched spinach leaves.

2   Cut salmon fillets into sixteen strips crossways to same size as perch strips. Sprinkle with remaining lemon juice and season to taste with white pepper.

3   Weave four strips of each fish into a square to form a checkerboard pattern on each piece of foil. Trim ends if necessary. Place a wire rack and 1$^{1}/_{4}$ inch (2.5 cm) of water in a large skillet, cover and bring to the boil. Place fish parcels on wire rack and steam for 6-8 minutes, or until fish flakes when tested with a fork.

4   To make sauce, melt half the butter in a saucepan and cook scallions, garlic and sage for 2 minutes. Add sorrel and cook over a low heat for 5 minutes, or until sorrel leaves are wilted. Add stock, bay leaf and wine. Bring to the boil and boil until mixture reduces by half. Remove bay leaf.

5   Place sauce in a food processor or blender and process until smooth. Pass through a fine sieve, then return to a clean saucepan. Stir in cream and cook over a low heat for 5 minutes. Whisk in small pieces of remaining butter. Season to taste with black pepper and set aside to keep warm. Serve fish squares with sauce.

Cut each perch fillet into four strips lengthways, sprinkle with lemon juice and season with white pepper. Wrap each strip in blanched spinach leaves.

Weave four strips of each fish into a square to form a checkerboard pattern on each piece of foil.

China Villeroy & Boch

FRESH HERB AND TOMATO SEAFOOD SOUP

A combination of fresh seafood and herbs helps to make this soup into the perfect one-pot meal.

Serves 6

- [ ] **3 tablespoons olive oil**
- [ ] **1 large red onion, thinly sliced**
- [ ] **2 cloves garlic, crushed**
- [ ] **8 cups (2 liters) fish stock**
- [ ] **1 can (16 oz/ 450 g) plum tomatoes, finely chopped and with their juice**
- [ ] **3 tablespoons white wine**
- [ ] **1/4 teaspoon ground saffron**
- [ ] **1/4 teaspoon Tabasco sauce**
- [ ] **1 teaspoon sugar**
- [ ] **freshly ground black pepper**
- [ ] **18 oz (500 g) thick white fish fillets, such as sea perch, skinned and cut into 1 1/4-inch (2.5 cm) cubes**
- [ ] **2/3 oz (160 mL) grated fresh Parmesan cheese**
- [ ] **3 egg yolks, lightly beaten with 1 tablespoon water**
- [ ] **1 tablespoon finely chopped fresh basil**
- [ ] **1 teaspoon finely chopped fresh lemon thyme**
- [ ] **12 mussels, scrubbed and de-bearded**
- [ ] **6 small squid, heads removed and bodies and leg sections cut into quarters**
- [ ] **12 jumbo shrimp, peeled and deveined**
- [ ] **2 large uncooked crabs, claws and legs removed and bodies halved**
- [ ] **1 tablespoon finely chopped fresh parsley**

1   Heat oil in a large saucepan and cook onion and garlic for 2 minutes. Add fish stock, tomatoes, wine, saffron, Tabasco, sugar, and black pepper to taste and cook over a low heat for 10 minutes.

2   Add fish and half the Parmesan cheese. Gradually whisk in egg yolk mixture and stir gently until combined.

3   Add basil, thyme, mussels, octopus, prawns and crab to soup, and cook over a low heat for 5 minutes. Serve garnished with parsley and remaining Parmesan cheese.

ASPARAGUS-FILLED FISH WITH PEPPERCORN SAUCE

Thick succulent fillets of fish, filled with scallops and asparagus and served with a creamy peppercorn sauce. This is a great do-ahead dish as the preparation of the fish fillets can be done earlier in the day.

Serves 6
Oven temperature 350°F (180°C)

- [ ] **6 thick white fish fillets, such as sea perch, skinned**
- [ ] **5 1/2 oz (155 g) scallops, chopped**
- [ ] **6 fresh asparagus spears, cut into 1 1/4-inch (2.5 cm) pieces and blanched**
- [ ] **3 tablespoons sour cream**
- [ ] **1 tablespoon snipped fresh chives**
- [ ] **freshly ground black pepper**

GREEN PEPPERCORN SAUCE
- [ ] **1 1/2 cups (355 mL) cream**
- [ ] **2 tablespoons green peppercorns, drained**
- [ ] **10 fresh basil leaves**

1   Cut a pocket in the side of each fish fillet, taking care not to cut right through fillet.

2   Place scallops, asparagus, sour cream, chives, and black pepper to taste in a bowl and mix to combine. Spoon mixture into pockets of fillets and secure with toothpicks. Place fish in a lightly oiled baking dish and cook for 10-15 minutes, or until flesh flakes when tested.

3   To make sauce, place cream, peppercorns and basil leaves in a skillet and cook over a low heat for 10-15 minutes, or until mixture thickens slightly. Remove basil from sauce. Spoon sauce over fish and serve immediately.

Fresh Herb and Tomato Seafood Soup, Asparagus-Filled Fish with Peppercorn Sauce, Smoked Salmon and Fresh Fruit Salad

SMOKED SALMON AND FRESH FRUIT SALAD

A salad of substance – a summer meal in itself. Accompany with crusty bread or rolls and you have a completely indulgent meal.

Serves 6

- [ ] **1 small papaya, or 2 small mangoes, peeled, seeded and cut into thick slices**
- [ ] **2 ripe avocados, pitted, peeled and cut into thick slices**
- [ ] **watercress**
- [ ] **24 slices smoked salmon**

DRESSING
- [ ] **2 tablespoons light olive oil**
- [ ] **3 tablespoons lime juice**
- [ ] **$^1/_2$ cup (120 mL) orange juice**
- [ ] **pulp of 3 passion fruit**
- [ ] **2 tablespoons sugar**
- [ ] **freshly ground black pepper**

1   Arrange papaya or mangoes, avocado, watercress and salmon attractively on six individual serving plates. Cover and refrigerate until required.

2   To make dressing, place oil, lime juice, orange juice, passion fruit pulp, sugar, and black pepper to taste in a screwtop jar. Shake well to combine. Just prior to serving pour dressing over salad.

FISHY TALES

❦   When buying fish freshness is vital. Look for fish with bright scales, firm flesh, bright clear eyes and moist, bright pink gills.

❦   Always purchase fish as close to cooking time as possible and from a fishmarket that has a good turnover.

❦   Any fish that smells is suspect. Do not buy or eat it as it is sure to lead to food poisoning.

China Bohemia Crystal

BANQUET FOR TWELVE

Take advantage of summer sunshine and lay the table for this indulgent smorgasbord – alfresco style. Much of the menu can be prepared ahead of time leaving only the final cooking and assembly to the last minute.

MENU

Smoked Salmon and
Potato Rounds

Coriander Mussels with
Lime Mayonnaise

Layered Pork Roast

Chicken Kebabs with
Raspberry Hollandaise

Peach Salad with
Mango Dressing

Summer Fruit Tartlets

SMOKED SALMON AND POTATO ROUNDS

The potato rounds and the topping for these delicious morsels can be prepared ahead of time. However, leave the final assembly until just prior to serving.

Makes 24

- ☐ **2 potatoes, peeled, finely grated and squeezed of excess liquid**
- ☐ **1 egg, lightly beaten**
- ☐ **freshly ground black pepper**
- ☐ **4 tablespoons butter**
- ☐ **3^1/2 oz (100 g) smoked salmon, cut into ^{1}/2-inch (1 cm) strips**
- ☐ **1 lime**

HORSERADISH CREAM
- ☐ **2 teaspoons white wine vinegar**
- ☐ **1 tablespoon prepared horseradish**
- ☐ **^{1}/2 teaspoon sugar**
- ☐ **freshly ground black pepper**
- ☐ **^{1}/2 cup (120 mL) heavy cream**

1   Place potato and egg in a bowl and mix well to combine. Season to taste with black pepper. Shape mixture into 24 balls and flatten slightly to form 1^1/4-inch (3 cm) rounds.

2   Melt 1^1/2 tablespoons butter in a skillet and cook 6 potato rounds until golden brown on both sides and cooked through. Remove from skillet and allow to cool on a wire rack. Repeat with remaining butter and mixture until all rounds are cooked.

3   To make Horseradish Cream, combine vinegar, horseradish and sugar in a mixing bowl. Season to taste with black pepper. Beat cream until stiff peaks form. Fold through horseradish mixture.

4   Peel lime with a vegetable peeler and cut rind into fine strips. Spread each potato round with horseradish cream and top with strips of salmon and lime.

COOK'S TIP

If prepared horseradish is not available for this recipe, ready-made horseradish relish, available at supermarkets and delicatessens, may be substituted.

CORIANDER MUSSELS WITH LIME MAYONNAISE

These delicious fritters can be prepared earlier in the day and final cooking done just prior to serving. The mayonnaise can be made 2-3 days in advance.

Makes 24

- ☐ **24 mussels, cleaned and de-bearded**
- ☐ **2 large bunches fresh coriander, stems removed**
- ☐ **4 tablespoons pine nuts**
- ☐ **6 cloves garlic, crushed**
- ☐ **4 tablespoons olive oil**
- ☐ **4 tablespoons grated fresh Parmesan cheese**
- ☐ **3 cups (705 mL) breadcrumbs made from stale bread**
- ☐ **freshly ground black pepper**
- ☐ **^{1}/2 cup (120 mL) all-purpose flour**
- ☐ **2 eggs, lightly beaten with 2 tablespoons milk**

LIME MAYONNAISE
- ☐ **3 egg yolks**
- ☐ **1 cup (240 mL) oil**
- ☐ **2 tablespoons lime juice**
- ☐ **freshly ground black pepper**

1   Cook mussels in a large saucepan of boiling water for 2-3 minutes, or until shells open. Remove mussels from water as they open to avoid overcooking. Discard any mussels that have not opened after 5 minutes cooking. Remove mussel meat from shells, drain on paper towels and set aside.

2   Place coriander leaves, pine nuts, garlic and 1 tablespoon oil in a food processor or blender and process until combined. With machine running, slowly add remaining oil. Transfer mixture to a bowl and mix in Parmesan cheese and breadcrumbs. Season to taste with black pepper.

3   Lightly dredge mussel meat with flour, dip in egg mixture and roll in coriander mixture, pressing firmly to coat mussels. Refrigerate for 30 minutes.

4   Place under preheated broiler and cook on both sides until pesto is golden.

5   To make mayonnaise, place egg yolks in a food processor or blender and with machine running, slowly pour in oil. Process until well combined and mixture thickens. Add lime juice and season to taste with black pepper. Serve with hot mussels.

LAYERED PORK ROAST

Serves 12
Oven temperature 350°F (180°C)

- ☐ **3 pork tenderloins, approximately 14 oz (400 g) each, trimmed of excess fat**
- ☐ **12 slices bacon, rind removed**
- ☐ **1 cup (240 mL) dry white wine**

SPINACH STUFFING
- ☐ **2 tablespoons butter**
- ☐ **^{1}/2 onion, chopped**
- ☐ **4^1/2 oz (125 g) button mushrooms, sliced**
- ☐ **9 oz (250 g) spinach, stalks removed and leaves shredded**
- ☐ **^{1}/2 teaspoon ground nutmeg**
- ☐ **^{1}/4 cup (60 mL) shelled pistachio nuts**
- ☐ **freshly ground black pepper**

TOMATO STUFFING
- ☐ **2 tablespoons butter**
- ☐ **^{1}/2 onion, sliced**
- ☐ **1 clove garlic, crushed**
- ☐ **2 tomatoes, peeled, seeded and finely chopped**
- ☐ **^{1}/2 apple, peeled, cored and finely chopped**
- ☐ **1 tablespoon tomato paste**
- ☐ **1 teaspoon sugar**
- ☐ **pulp of 1 passion fruit**
- ☐ **^{3}/4 cup (180 mL) breadcrumbs made from stale bread**
- ☐ **freshly ground black pepper**

1   To make Spinach Stuffing, melt butter in a skillet and cook onion for 4-5 minutes or until soft. Add mushrooms and cook for 4 minutes longer. Stir in spinach and cook until wilted. Remove from heat and mix in nutmeg and pistachio nuts. Season to taste with black pepper.

2   To make Tomato Stuffing, melt butter in a skillet and cook onion and garlic for 4-5 minutes or until soft. Add tomatoes, apple, tomato paste, sugar and passion fruit pulp and cook for 3 minutes longer. Stir in breadcrumbs and season to taste with black pepper.

3   Slit each pork tenderloin lengthways, three-quarters of the way through. Open out each piece of meat so that it is as flat as possible. Top one piece with spinach mixture and place a second piece on top. Spread with tomato mixture and top with remaining tenderloin.

4   Wrap bacon around meat and tie with string to secure roll. Place on a roasting rack in a roasting pan and pour wine into pan. Bake 1^1/2-2 hours, or until cooked through, basting frequently with juices in pan. Allow to cool completely.

CHICKEN KEBABS WITH RASPBERRY HOLLANDAISE

Succulent strips of chicken grilled and topped with a fruity hollandaise. If you are serving this meal outdoors, why not cook these kebabs on the barbecue.

Makes 12

- ☐ **3 whole chicken breasts, skinned, boned and split**

RASPBERRY MARINADE
- ☐ **¹/₂ cup (120 mL) olive oil**
- ☐ **1¹/₂ tablespoons raspberry vinegar**
- ☐ **2 teaspoons Framboise (raspberry liqueur)**
- ☐ **1 clove garlic, crushed**

RASPBERRY HOLLANDAISE SAUCE
- ☐ **3 egg yolks**
- ☐ **3 tablespoons water**
- ☐ **13 tablespoons butter, clarified and cooled to tepid**
- ☐ **¹/₂ pint (240 mL) raspberries, puréed**
- ☐ **1 teaspoon raspberry vinegar**
- ☐ **1 tablespoon finely chopped fresh basil**
- ☐ **freshly ground black pepper**

1 To make marinade, combine oil, vinegar, liqueur and garlic in a screwtop jar and shake well to combine.
2 Cut chicken into thin strips and thread on to twelve oiled wooden skewers. Place into a shallow dish and pour marinade over. Cover and refrigerate for 2 hours or overnight.
3 To make sauce, whisk egg yolks and water in top of a double saucepan, over simmering water, until mixture is light in colour. Cook over a low heat, whisking constantly until mixture becomes thick enough to leave a trail – take care not to overheat. Remove saucepan from heat and add butter a little at a time, whisking continuously until sauce thickens, then add remaining butter in a steady stream. Stir through raspberry purée, raspberry vinegar and basil. Season to taste with black pepper. Set aside and keep warm.
4 Cook kebabs under a preheated broiler for 5-10 minutes, or until browned and cooked through, basting frequently with marinade. Serve with sauce.

PEACH SALAD WITH MANGO DRESSING

Bibb lettuce and watercress create the base for this colorful salad of summer fruits.

Serves 12

- ☐ **6 peaches, peeled and pitted**
- ☐ **freshly ground black pepper**
- ☐ **3 cups (705 mL) watercress**
- ☐ **2 bibb lettuces, leaves separated and torn into pieces**
- ☐ **1 cup (240 mL) macadamia nuts, roughly chopped**

MANGO DRESSING
- ☐ **1 large ripe mango, pitted, peeled and chopped**
- ☐ **2 tablespoons olive oil**
- ☐ **2 tablespoons white wine vinegar**
- ☐ **1 tablespoon snipped fresh chives**

1 To make dressing, place mango, oil and vinegar in a food processor or blender and process until smooth. Stir in chives.
2 Sprinkle peaches liberally with black pepper and arrange with watercress, lettuce and macadamia nuts on a serving platter. Pour dressing over.

SUMMER FRUIT TARTLETS

The perfect finish to the perfect meal. Use any fresh fruit of your choice in these delicately delicious tartlets.

Makes 12
Oven temperature 425°F (220°C)

- ☐ **1¹/₂ cups (355 mL) all-purpose flour, sifted**
- ☐ **¹/₄ teaspoon baking powder**
- ☐ **1 tablespoon sugar**
- ☐ **5 tablespoons chilled butter, chopped**
- ☐ **1 egg yolk, lightly beaten**
- ☐ **2 tablespoons iced water**

FILLING
- ☐ **9 oz (250 g) mascarpone; about 1¹/₄ cups (300 mL)**
- ☐ **2 tablespoons confectioners sugar, sifted**
- ☐ **2 teaspoons ground cinnamon**
- ☐ **2 teaspoons ground mixed spice**
- ☐ **1 tablespoon Kirsch (cherry brandy)**
- ☐ **¹/₂ pint (240 mL) blueberries**
- ☐ **¹/₂ pint (240 mL) redcurrants**

1 Combine flour, baking powder and sugar in a mixing bowl. Rub in butter, using fingertips, until mixture resembles coarse breadcrumbs. Stir in egg yolk and enough water to mix to a firm dough, using a dull knife. Knead dough on a lightly floured surface until smooth. Wrap in plastic wrap and refrigerate for 1 hour.
2 Roll out pastry and line 12 individual 4-inch (10 cm) tart pans. Prick bases and sides with a fork, line with parchment paper and dried beans, and blind bake for 5 minutes. Remove baking beans and paper and bake for 5-8 minutes longer or until golden. Set aside to cool.
3 To make the filling, place mascarpone, confectioners sugar, cinnamon, mixed spice and Kirsch in a mixing bowl and beat until smooth. Cover and refrigerate until required. Just prior to serving, spoon mascarpone mixture into cooled pastry cases and top with blueberries and redcurrants.

FAST FEASTS

When time is short and aspirations high, try one of these fast and fabulous meals. They all taste wonderful and some look and taste as if they have taken hours to prepare. Perfect for unexpected guests, or for an easy indulgence.

❦

BANANA MOUSSE

Light, fluffy and creamy, this mousse takes next to no time to make and is the perfect finish to any meal.

Serves 8

- ☐ **3 eggs, separated**
- ☐ **$^1/_2$ cup (120 mL) sugar**
- ☐ **4 tablespoons cream of coconut**
- ☐ **3 small ripe bananas, peeled and chopped**
- ☐ **1 tablespoon lemon juice**
- ☐ **1 teaspoon ground cinnamon**
- ☐ **1 tablespoon Marsala**
- ☐ **3 teaspoons unflavored gelatin dissolved in 3 tablespoons hot water and cooled**
- ☐ **1 cup (240 mL) heavy cream**

1   Place egg yolks and sugar in a mixing bowl and beat until thick and creamy.
2   Place cream of coconut, bananas, lemon juice, cinnamon and Marsala in a food processor or blender and process until smooth. Blend cooled gelatin mixture into egg yolk mixture, then stir in coconut mixture.
3   Place cream in a bowl and beat until soft peaks form, then fold through banana mixture. Beat egg whites until stiff peaks form and fold through banana mixture. Spoon into eight individual serving glasses and refrigerate until firm.

❦

SMOKED SALMON BAGUETTE

A happy marriage of all the best ingredients, this filled baguette is a meal in itself.

Serves 4

- ☐ **1 long French baguette**
- ☐ **2 teaspoons Dijon mustard**
- ☐ **1 teaspoon lemon juice**
- ☐ **3 hard-boiled eggs, peeled and sliced**
- ☐ **2 tablespoons capers, drained and chopped**
- ☐ **11 oz (315 g) smoked salmon slices**
- ☐ **1 red onion, thinly sliced**
- ☐ **1$^1/_2$ cups (355 mL) watercress**
- ☐ **freshly ground black pepper**

1   Slice baguette through horizontally and remove some of the centre. Combine mustard and lemon juice and spread over inside of bread.
2   Place eggs on mustard mixture on bottom half of baguette, top with capers, salmon, onion and watercress. Season to taste with black pepper and cover with bread top. Tie at intervals with string and cut into four.

Smoked Salmon Baguette, Banana Mousse

China Incorporated Agencies

🐚
STIR-FRY NOODLES WITH SEAFOOD

The flavors and ingredients of the Orient combine to make this fast feast. Vary the vegetables according to what is available and how indulgent you feel.

Serves 4

- [ ] **13 oz (375 g) fresh egg noodles**
- [ ] **2 tablespoons sesame oil**
- [ ] **1 clove garlic, crushed**
- [ ] **2 small red chillies, finely chopped**
- [ ] **1 teaspoon grated fresh ginger**
- [ ] **18 oz (500 g) jumbo shrimp, peeled and deveined**
- [ ] **9 oz (250 g) scallops**
- [ ] **9 oz (250 g) calamari, sliced**
- [ ] **1/2 red pepper, cut into thin strips**
- [ ] **2 oz (60 g) snow peas, cut diagonally into 1-inch (2.5 cm) pieces**
- [ ] **9 oz (250 g) asparagus, cut into 1-inch (2.5 cm) pieces**
- [ ] **1 tablespoon finely shredded fresh basil**
- [ ] **2 tablespoons sesame seeds, toasted**

SAUCE
- [ ] **1 tablespoon cornstarch**
- [ ] **1 tablespoon sugar**
- [ ] **3 tablespoons tomato sauce**
- [ ] **1 teaspoon oyster sauce**
- [ ] **1 tablespoon Worcestershire sauce**
- [ ] **1 cup (240 mL) water**

1   Place noodles in a large saucepan of boiling water and cook for 3 minutes or until tender. Drain, then rinse under hot water. Spread out on paper towels.

2   Heat oil in a skillet or wok and cook garlic, chillies and ginger for 1 minute. Stir in shrimp, scallops, calamari, red pepper, snow peas, asparagus and basil and cook for 2-3 minutes, or until shrimp just turn pink. Add noodles to pan and stir-fry for 1-2 minutes, or until heated through.

3   To make sauce, combine cornstarch, sugar, tomato sauce, oyster sauce, Worcestershire sauce and water. Pour into pan and cook over a medium heat until sauce boils and thickens. Sprinkle with sesame seeds and serve immediately.

Stir-Fry Noodles with Seafood

TIPS FOR FAST FEASTING
🐚   A well-stocked pantry means that you can 'dress up' otherwise everyday foods quickly and easily.

🐚   A good range of dried herbs and spices and some fresh herbs grown in your garden or in a window box can quickly transform a basic dish into a taste sensation.

🐚   Look out for new Asian and Middle Eastern spice combinations.

🐚   Keep a variety of interesting oils and vinegars for marinades and dressings that will add punch to basic steak, chops or chicken.

🐚   Most dressings and marinades keep well and can be made in advance.

🐚   Do not be afraid to use convenience foods for a fast and fabulous meal. There is an excellent range of sauces, soups, stocks and condiments available that can enhance the simplest of foods.

CHICKEN AND CHEESE FOCACCIA SANDWICHES

Italian focaccia bread makes a great alternative to ordinary bread when you want something more substantial. Serve these delicious sandwiches with a green salad for a complete meal.

Serves 4

- [ ] **4 pieces focaccia bread, split horizontally**
- [ ] **1 whole chicken breast, skinned, boned and split**
- [ ] **1 tablespoon butter**
- [ ] **1 tablespoon olive oil**
- [ ] **1 clove garlic, unpeeled**
- [ ] **4 slices ham**
- [ ] **8 slices Swiss cheese**
- [ ] **1 tablespoon snipped fresh chives**
- [ ] **1 tablespoon finely chopped fresh dill**
- [ ] **freshly ground black pepper**

1 Trim chicken breasts. Slice each half-breast horizontally to give 2 slices. Pound each slice to flatten.

2 Heat butter, oil and unpeeled clove garlic in a large heavy-based skillet. Cook chicken, 2 slices at a time, for 1-2 minutes each side.

3 Place a slice of chicken on the bottom half of each focaccia. Top with a slice of ham and a slice of cheese. Place a slice of cheese on top half of each piece of focaccia.

4 Place focaccia halves under a hot broiler and cook until cheese melts. Sprinkle chives and dill on bottom halves. Season to taste with black pepper. Place top halves of focaccia on bottom halves and serve immediately.

RED PEPPERED BEEF

A quick and easy Chinese dish with a medley of flavors and textures, which is sure to be popular. Serve with boiled or steamed rice and a side dish of fresh steamed vegetables.

Serves 4

- [ ] **18 oz (500 g) top round steak, cut into thin strips**
- [ ] **2 teaspoons cornstarch**
- [ ] **2 tablespoons soy sauce**
- [ ] **2 tablespoons peanut oil**
- [ ] **2 red peppers, cut into thin strips**
- [ ] **1 small red chilli, finely chopped**
- [ ] **4 green onions, cut into 2-inch (5 cm) lengths**
- [ ] **1 clove garlic, crushed**
- [ ] **2 teaspoons grated fresh ginger**
- [ ] **1 teaspoon sugar**
- [ ] **2 tablespoons dry sherry**

1 Sprinkle meat strips with cornstarch and 2 tablespoons soy sauce. Toss to coat and set aside to stand for 5 minutes.

2 Heat 1 tablespoon oil in a skillet or wok, add red peppers, chilli, green onions, garlic and ginger and cook for 2-3 minutes. Remove from pan and set aside.

3 Heat remaining oil in wok or skillet and stir-fry meat for 2-3 minutes. Return pepper mixture to pan. Combine remaining soy sauce, sugar and sherry and pour into pan. Stir-fry for 1 minute longer, then serve immediately.

Chicken and Cheese Focaccia Sandwiches, Red Peppered Beef

China Noritake

SPINACH RAVIOLI WITH MASCARPONE SAUCE

These classic stuffed pasta shapes take on a new dimension in this recipe. The mascarpone sauce also goes well with other pasta.

Serves 2

- [ ] **18 oz (500 g) fresh spinach ravioli**

MASCARPONE SAUCE
- [ ] **2 teaspoons vegetable oil**
- [ ] **3 oz (90 g) pancetta, finely chopped**
- [ ] **$^3/_4$ cup (180 mL) chicken stock**
- [ ] **$6^1/_2$ oz (185 g) mascarpone**
- [ ] **8 sun-dried tomatoes, chopped**
- [ ] **1 tablespoon finely chopped fresh basil**
- [ ] **1 tablespoon snipped fresh chives**
- [ ] **freshly ground black pepper**
- [ ] **grated fresh Parmesan cheese**

1   Cook ravioli in boiling water in a large saucepan for 4-5 minutes or until 'al dente'. Drain and set aside to keep warm.
2   To make sauce, heat oil in a small saucepan and cook pancetta for 2-3 minutes. Stir in stock, mascarpone and sun-dried tomatoes, and simmer for 5 minutes, or until sauce reduces and thickens. Stir in basil, chives, and black pepper to taste. Spoon sauce over pasta, toss to coat, sprinkle with Parmesan cheese and serve immediately.

LIQUEUR STRAWBERRY DESSERT

This quick and easy dessert looks and tastes as if it has taken hours to prepare – don't let on just how little time it really takes.

Serves 4

- [ ] **$^1/_2$ pint (240 mL) strawberries, hulled and sliced lengthways**
- [ ] **4 tablespoons Grand Marnier (orange liqueur)**
- [ ] **3 eggs, separated**
- [ ] **1 tablespoon sugar**
- [ ] **9 oz (250 g) mascarpone**
- [ ] **$3^1/_2$ oz (100 g) amaretti cookies, crushed**

1   Place strawberries and liqueur in a bowl and set aside to macerate for 30 minutes.
2   Place egg yolks and mascarpone in a bowl and beat until smooth. Beat egg whites until soft peaks form, then gradually beat in sugar. Fold egg white mixture into mascarpone mixture.
3   Divide half the mascarpone mixture between four individual serving dishes, sprinkle half the cookies over mixture then top with strawberries and remaining mascarpone mixture. Finally sprinkle with remaining cookies. Cover with plastic wrap and refrigerate until required.

COMBINATION NOODLE SOUP

A Chinese-style main meal soup that uses canned broth as its base, is a quick and tasty dish when time is short.

Serves 6

- [ ] **2 teaspoons peanut oil**
- [ ] **1 onion, finely chopped**
- [ ] **1 red pepper, finely chopped**
- [ ] **2 cans (16 oz/450 g each) chicken broth**
- [ ] **2 cups (470 mL) water**
- [ ] **1 chicken breast, boned and skinned, cooked and thinly sliced**
- [ ] **13 oz (375 g) Chinese barbecued pork filet, thinly sliced**
- [ ] **12 medium shrimp, peeled and deveined**
- [ ] **$3^1/_2$ oz (100 g) rice noodles, cooked**
- [ ] **3 oz (75 g) oyster mushrooms, sliced**
- [ ] **3 oz (75 g) canned bamboo shoots, sliced**
- [ ] **4 lettuce leaves, shredded**
- [ ] **1 tablespoon finely chopped fresh coriander**
- [ ] **freshly ground black pepper**

1   Heat oil in a large saucepan and cook onion and red pepper for 5 minutes or until soft.
2   Add chicken broth and water and bring to the boil. Reduce heat and add chicken, pork, shrimp, rice noodles, mushrooms and bamboo shoots. Simmer for 5 minutes, or until shrimp turn pink and are cooked. Stir in lettuce, coriander, and black pepper to taste. Serve immediately.

Spinach Ravioli with Mascarpone Sauce, Liqueur Strawberry Dessert, Combination Noodle Soup

QUICK AND CASUAL

This section is full of recipes suitable for quick, casual meals. Many can be cooked on the grill or under the broiler and are suitable for both experienced and inexperienced cooks.

CHILLI SEAFOOD SKEWERS

When cooking on a grill, oil it so that the food does not stick to it.

Serves 4

- ☐ **8 bamboo skewers, oiled**
- ☐ **8 jumbo shrimp, peeled and deveined with tails left intact**
- ☐ **8 sea scallops**
- ☐ **1 large white fish fillet, cut into 3^1/4 x ^{3}/4-inch (8 x 2 cm) cubes**
- ☐ **1 large salmon fillet, cut into 3^1/4 x ^{3}/4-inch (8 x 2 cm) cubes**
- ☐ **8 mussels, removed from shells**

MARINADE
- ☐ **4 tablespoons vegetable oil**
- ☐ **3 red chillies, finely chopped**
- ☐ **2 cloves garlic, crushed**
- ☐ **2 tablespoons lemon juice**

1　Push point of a wooden skewer through tail end of a shrimp. Thread on a scallop and then push skewer through top of shrimp. Thread a piece of white fish, a mussel and a piece of salmon onto skewer. Repeat with remaining seafood and skewers.

2　To make marinade, combine oil, chillies, garlic and lemon juice in a bowl. Place skewers on a hot grill or under a hot broiler and brush with marinade. Cook, turning frequently, until seafood changes color and is cooked through. Serve immediately.

Chilli Seafood Skewers, Thai Lime Cornish Hens (page 48)

China Bohemia Crystal

THAI LIME CORNISH HENS

Evoke the taste of Thailand, with tender Cornish Hens marinated in lime juice, coriander and coconut milk.

Serves 4

☐ **4 Cornish Game hens**

MARINADE
☐ **3 tablespoons lime juice**
☐ **2 tablespoons chopped fresh coriander**
☐ **1 cup (240 mL) coconut milk**
☐ **1 red chilli, chopped**
☐ **2 tablespoons honey**
☐ **freshly ground black pepper**

1 Cut Cornish hens down middle of backs and flatten. Thread a skewer through wings and a skewer through legs of each hen.

2 To make marinade, place lime juice, coriander, coconut milk, chilli, honey, and black pepper to taste in a large baking dish. Mix to combine. Place Cornish hens flesh side down in marinade. Cover and refrigerate for 4 hours or overnight.

3 Cook on a hot grill or under a hot broiler, basting frequently with marinade. Cook 15 minutes each side, or until tender and cooked through.

RAINBOW TROUT WITH DILL BUTTER

Trout is delicious and versatile. Served with a herb butter, it makes a fast and impressive main dish cooked on the grill or in the oven.

Serves 4
Oven temperature 350°F (180°C)

☐ **4 rainbow trout, cleaned**

DILL BUTTER
☐ **6 tablespoons butter, softened**
☐ **2 tablespoons chopped fresh dill**
☐ **1 clove garlic, crushed**
☐ **2 teaspoons grated lemon zest**

1 To make Dill Butter, place butter, dill, garlic and lemon zest in a bowl and mix until combined.

2 Place trout on individual pieces of foil large enough to enclose trout. Spread each trout with Dill Butter and wrap foil around trout to enclose. Place parcels on grill and cook for 10 minutes each side, or bake in oven for 15 minutes, or until fish flakes when tested.

Right: Italian Beef Rolls, Spicy Mint Lamb Riblets
Below: Rainbow Trout with Dill Butter

China Noritake

China Villeroy & Boch

ITALIAN BEEF ROLLS

*Tender slices of steak wrapped around
a cheese and tomato filling.*

Serves 4

- [ ] **4 thin bottom round steaks**
- [ ] **8 spinach leaves, stalks removed**
- [ ] **16 cherry tomatoes**

CHEESE FILLING
- [ ] **$^1/_2$ cup (120 mL) grated mozzarella cheese**
- [ ] **$^1/_2$ cup (120 mL) ricotta cheese**
- [ ] **1 tablespoon chopped fresh parsley**
- [ ] **freshly ground black pepper**

1   Trim all visible fat from meat. Place meat on a board, cover with plastic wrap and pound, using a mallet, until thin. Divide spinach into four portions and spread in a layer over each piece of steak.

2   To make filling, combine mozzarella, ricotta, parsley, and black pepper to taste. Spread over spinach, then place cherry tomatoes across middle of filling and roll up. Secure with toothpicks. Grill, turning on a hot, oiled plate for 10 minutes, or until cooked through.

SPICY MINT LAMB RIBLETS

*This recipe uses tender young lamb
riblets rather than pork or beef ribs,
making a quickly prepared dish. Serve
with a green salad and crusty bread for
a complete meal.*

Serves 4
Oven temperature 350°F (180°C)

- [ ] **2 lamb breasts, cut into riblets**

MARINADE
- [ ] **$^1/_2$ cup (120 mL) mint jelly**
- [ ] **2 tablespoons Worcestershire sauce**
- [ ] **1 teaspoon chilli powder**
- [ ] **2 teaspoons finely chopped fresh rosemary**
- [ ] **freshly ground black pepper**

1   To make marinade, place mint jelly, Worcestershire sauce, chilli powder, rosemary, and black pepper to taste in a bowl and mix to combine. Place riblets in a large baking dish and pour marinade over. Cover and refrigerate overnight.

2   Remove cover and bake riblets for 20 minutes, or until cooked through and tender. Transfer ribs to a hot grill or broiler and cook for 5-10 minutes longer, or until browned. Brush frequently with marinade during cooking.

49

FLAPJACK STACKS

Warm flapjacks with maple syrup – what better brunch dish?

Makes 10

- ☐ **1 cup (240 mL) self-rising flour, sifted**
- ☐ **2 tablespoons sugar**
- ☐ **1 egg, lightly beaten**
- ☐ **³/₄ cup (180 mL) buttermilk**
- ☐ **maple syrup**

1   Place flour and sugar in a bowl. Mix in egg and buttermilk until smooth. Cook tablespoons of mixture in a heated greased heavy-based skillet. Turn flapjacks when bubbles appear on the surface.

2   Place flapjacks in a stack and top with maple syrup.

MACADAMIA TART

The combination of macadamia nuts and spices tastes wonderful in this easy-to-make baked tart. Eaten hot, warm or cold, it is absolutely delicious and would make the perfect dessert for a grill.

Serves 12
Oven temperature 425°F (220°C)

SPICED PASTRY
- ☐ **1¹/₂ cups (355 mL) all-purpose flour, sifted**
- ☐ **¹/₄ teaspoon baking powder**
- ☐ **1 teaspoon ground mixed spice**
- ☐ **1 tablespoon sugar**
- ☐ **9 tablespoons chilled butter, chopped**
- ☐ **1 egg yolk, lightly beaten**
- ☐ **1 tablespoon iced water**

MACADAMIA FILLING
- ☐ **4 tablespoons butter**
- ☐ **¹/₂ cup (120 mL) brown sugar**
- ☐ **1 teaspoon vanilla extract**
- ☐ **3 eggs**
- ☐ **³/₄ cup (180 mL) light corn syrup**
- ☐ **2 tablespoons all-purpose flour, sifted**
- ☐ **1 teaspoon ground mixed spice**
- ☐ **1 teaspoon ground cinnamon**
- ☐ **1¹/₃ cups (320 mL) roasted macadamia nuts, roughly chopped**

1   To make pastry, combine flour, baking powder, mixed spice and sugar in a mixing bowl. Rub in butter with fingertips until mixture resembles coarse breadcrumbs. Stir in egg yolk and enough water to mix to a firm dough, using a blunt knife. Knead

dough lightly on a floured surface until smooth. Wrap in plastic wrap and refrigerate for 1 hour.

2   Roll out pastry and line a greased 9³/₄-inch (25 cm) tart pan. Prick base and sides with a fork and line with parchment paper and uncooked beans. Blind bake for 5 minutes, then remove beans and paper and cook pastry for 8 minutes longer. Set aside to cool.

3   To make filling, beat butter, sugar and vanilla essence until light and fluffy. Add eggs one at a time beating well after each addition. Fold through corn syrup, flour, mixed spice, cinnamon and macadamia nuts. Spoon filling into tart shell and bake at 320°F (160°C) for 35-40 minutes or until firm.

Flapjack Stacks, Macadamia Tart

China Incorporated Agencies

Smoked Salmon Brioches

❦

SMOKED SALMON BRIOCHES

If brioches are unavailable, you might like to use small bread rolls for this recipe.

Serves 6

☐   **6 small brioches**

SALMON FILLING
☐   **3¹/₂ oz (200 g) cream cheese**
☐   **4 tablespoons sour cream**
☐   **1 tablespoon capers, chopped**
☐   **2 teaspoons chopped fresh dill**
☐   **6 slices smoked salmon, chopped**
☐   **2 teaspoons lemon juice**

1   Cut top from brioches, scoop out centre and discard. Set brioches aside.

2   To make filling, place cream cheese and sour cream in a bowl and beat until light and smooth. Fold through capers, dill, salmon and lemon juice. Spoon filling into brioches and replace with tops.

TABLE SETTING

Simple household items, such as bed sheets and ribbons, can inexpensively transform any table into a lavish setting. All it takes is a little know-how.

AN INDULGENT TABLE

Our round table for four has a diameter of 48 inches (122 cm).

MATERIALS
- ☐ **1 white Queen size sheet**
- ☐ **1 patterned Queen size sheet**
- ☐ **double-sided tape**
- ☐ **4 lengths of 2-inch (5 cm) wide ribbon, each 1^1/2 yards (1.40 m)**
- ☐ **4 small gifts**
- ☐ **pink wrapping paper**
- ☐ **3 yards (3 m) of ^{1}/2-inch (1 cm) wide ribbon**
- ☐ **4 napkins (paper or linen)**

METHOD
1   Press both sheets well to remove any creases. Cover table with white sheet. To make the sheet hang evenly on the round table, fold each corner under to the wrong side and tape it up with double-sided tape.
2   Cover white sheet with patterned sheet. Fold point of each corner inside to allow white sheet to extend below. Tape up with double-sided tape. Gather each corner of pattern sheet and tie with one length of 1^1/2 yards (1.40 m) ribbon. Tie ribbon into a bow. Neaten ends of bow by cutting a 'fish-tail'.
3   Wrap individual gifts in pink wrapping paper and tie with ^{1}/2-inch (1 cm) wide ribbon. Place at each place setting.
4   Fold napkins and position at each place.

FINAL DETAILS
The napkins have been folded to form what is known as a Bishop's Hat
1   Fold napkin into a triangle. Centre of triangle points down.
2   Fold right-hand and left-hand corners down to centre point.
3   Fold top corner down 4 inches (10 cm), towards bottom point.
4   Fold folded point back to upper edge.
5   Turn napkin over. Fold bottom edges to overlap and tuck inside at back.
6   Stand napkin and turn down two outer points.

The centrepiece for this table is a silver teapot – a family treasure – filled with tiny bud roses. A handmade doily complements the arrangement.

A small gift of soap for each person is a pleasure to receive as well as delicately scenting the room. Other gift ideas are small pouches of potpourri tied with a pretty ribbon, or an individual flower picked fresh from your garden.

NOSTALGIA FOOD

These are the meals that we all dream about. They are hearty and delicious, evoking memories of childhood days – the meals that your family and friends will love you for.

PEACH BREAD AND BUTTER CARAMEL DESSERT

Caramel poured into the base of the baking dish adds a delicious flavor to this traditional English dessert. Baking it in a pan of hot water ensures a smooth, creamy custard.

Serves 8
Oven temperature 350°F (180°C)

- ☐ **6 peaches, peeled, pitted and sliced**
- ☐ **3 tablespoons butter, softened**
- ☐ **12 slices white bread, crusts removed**
- ☐ **3 teaspoons cinnamon**

CARAMEL
- ☐ **³/₄ cup (180 mL) sugar**
- ☐ **³/₄ cup (180 mL) water**

BENEDICTINE CUSTARD
- ☐ **3 eggs**
- ☐ **²/₃ cup (160 mL) sugar**
- ☐ **1 cup (240 mL) milk, scalded**
- ☐ **1 cup (240 mL) cream, scalded**
- ☐ **2 tablespoons Benedictine**

1   To make caramel, place sugar and water in a small saucepan and cook, stirring over a low heat until sugar dissolves. Increase heat and simmer until caramel is a golden color. Pour caramel into base of a well greased 9³/₄-inch (25 cm) round ovenproof dish.

2   Poach or microwave peaches until just tender, drain well and set aside.

3   To make custard, place eggs and sugar in a bowl and whisk to combine. Whisk in milk, cream and Benedictine and mix to combine. Butter bread on one side, then cut into triangles.

4   Place a layer of bread in base of ovenproof dish then top with a layer of peaches and sprinkle with cinnamon. Repeat layers, until bread, peaches and cinnamon are all used, ending with a bread layer. Pour custard evenly over the layers. Bake for 50-60 minutes, or until custard is set. Stand for 15 minutes before turning out and serving.

Peach Bread and Butter Caramel Dessert, Standing Rib Roast with Horseradish (page 58)

China Wedgewood *Silverware* R.P. Symons

COCONUT AND ALMOND LAMB CURRY

Flavored with fragrant spices, this curry has a rich creamy texture. To make it really special, decorate with gold leaf, available from Asian foodstores.

Serves 6

- ☐ **3 cloves garlic, peeled**
- ☐ **1 teaspoon grated fresh ginger**
- ☐ **$^1/_3$ cup (80 mL) blanched almonds**
- ☐ **2 tablespoons shredded coconut, toasted**
- ☐ **3 fresh red chillies, chopped**
- ☐ **2 tablespoons ghee or oil**
- ☐ **1 large onion, finely chopped**
- ☐ **1 teaspoon ground cumin**
- ☐ **1 teaspoon ground cardamom**
- ☐ **$^1/_2$ teaspoon ground fennel seed**
- ☐ **4 whole cloves or $^1/_4$ teaspoon ground cloves**
- ☐ **1 teaspoon black mustard seeds**
- ☐ **2 tablespoons freshly chopped coriander or mint**
- ☐ **2 tomatoes, peeled and chopped**
- ☐ **$3^1/_4$ pounds ($1^1/_2$ kg) boneless leg or shoulder lamb, cubed**
- ☐ **1 cup (240 mL) beef stock**
- ☐ **$^1/_2$ cup (120 mL) cream of coconut**
- ☐ **1 teaspoon garam masala**
- ☐ **1 tablespoon slivered almonds, toasted**
- ☐ **1 small envelope edible gold leaf (optional)**

1   Place garlic, ginger, almonds, coconut and chillies in a food processor or blender with a little water and process to form a smooth paste.

2   Heat ghee or oil in a large heavy-based skillet and cook onion and almond paste over a low heat for 2-3 minutes, stirring occasionally. Add cumin, cardamom, fennel, cloves, mustard seeds, and coriander or mint. Cook, stirring, for 4-5 minutes longer. Stir in tomatoes, mashing well to form a pulpy mixture. Add lamb and cook over a medium-high heat, stirring well to coat meat with spice mixture. Stir in stock and bring to the boil.

3   Reduce heat, cover and simmer for 1-$1^1/_2$ hours, or until lamb is tender and liquid reduces and thickens. Stir occasionally to prevent curry from sticking to pan.

4   Pour in cream of coconut, sprinkle with garam marsala and cook, stirring, for 5 minutes longer. Just prior to serving sprinkle with slivered almonds, and flakes of gold leaf, if using.

SERVING SUGGESTION

Serve this tasty lamb curry with boiled basmati rice and a selection of sambals, such as chopped tomato and onion with mint or basil; chopped cucumber with yogurt and chopped dill; sliced banana or pineapple sprinkled with coconut; chilli pickles; or a hot mango chutney.

Accompany with poppadums, or an Indian bread such as naan or chapati.

Above: Steak with Seeded Mustard Sauce, Gourmet Barbecue Sausages
Right: Stilton Soup, Coconut and Almond Lamb Curry

STILTON SOUP

A creamy soup that takes only about half an hour to prepare.

Serves 6

- ☐ **2 tablespoons butter**
- ☐ **1 onion, finely chopped**
- ☐ **3 leeks, washed, trimmed and cut into $^1/_2$-inch (1 cm) thick slices**
- ☐ **3 cups (720 mL) chicken stock**
- ☐ **1 bouquet garni**
- ☐ **$1^1/_2$ tablespoons cornstarch blended with 3 tablespoons milk**
- ☐ **$1^1/_2$ cups (375 mL) milk**
- ☐ **freshly ground black pepper**
- ☐ **7 oz (200 g) Stilton cheese, trimmed of crust, crumbled**
- ☐ **1 tablespoon finely chopped fresh parsley**

1   Melt butter in a large saucepan and cook onion over a medium heat, for 5 minutes or until soft. Add leeks and cook for 5 minutes longer.

2   Stir in stock and bouquet garni. Bring to the boil, then reduce heat and simmer uncovered for 20 minutes.

3   Stir cornstarch mixture and milk into soup and bring slowly to a simmer, stirring constantly. Stir cheese into soup then remove from heat and stir until cheese is completely melted and soup is creamy. Season to taste with black pepper. Ladle into soup bowls, sprinkle with parsley and serve immediately.

STEAK WITH SEEDED MUSTARD SAUCE

Serves 2

- ☐ **2 boneless sirloin or filet steaks, $^1/_2$-$1^1/_2$ inches (3-4 cm) thick**

MUSTARD SAUCE
- ☐ **1 tablespoon wholegrain mustard**
- ☐ **1 cup (240 mL) cream**
- ☐ **freshly ground black pepper**
- ☐ **lemon juice to taste**

1   Sauté or broil steaks until cooked to your liking. If sautéing steaks, remove meat from pan and keep warm. Drain meat juices from pan, leaving about 1 tablespoon in pan. If broiling steaks, melt a little butter in a small skillet.

2   To make sauce, stir mustard into pan and cook for 1 minute. Pour in cream and cook over high heat, stirring well until sauce reduces and becomes thick and glossy. Season to taste with black pepper and lemon juice. Spoon over steak and serve immediately.

GOURMET BARBECUE SAUSAGES

Choose from the specialty sausages available at supermarkets and butchers' shops to add an individual touch.

Serves 4
- ☐ **8 thick sausages**
- ☐ **$^1/_2$ cup (120 mL) oyster sauce**
- ☐ **2 tablespoons wholegrain mustard**
- ☐ **24 fresh oysters, drained**

1   Place sausages in a large saucepan of cold water and bring slowly to the boil. Drain and allow sausages to cool.

2   Brush sausages with oyster sauce and broil or grill, brushing frequently with oyster sauce, until browned and heated through. Cut each sausage halfway through, along one side. Spread a little mustard in each sausage and fill with oysters. Brush with oyster sauce and return to grill or broiler to heat through.

STANDING RIB ROAST WITH HORSERADISH

In this Master Class you learn how to cook the perfect roast meal and how to make individual Yorkshire Puddings to add that finishing touch.

Serves 6
Oven temperature 375°F (190°C)

- ☐ 4^1/$_2$ **pounds (2 kg) prime rib of beef on the bone**
- ☐ 3^1/$_2$ **tablespoons butter, softened**
- ☐ **4 tablespoons vegetable oil**
- ☐ **freshly ground black pepper**
- ☐ **6 potatoes, peeled and halved**
- ☐ **3 carrots, peeled and halved**
- ☐ **6 small Spanish onions, peeled**
- ☐ **3 parsnips, peeled and halved**
- ☐ ^{2}/$_3$ **cup (160 mL) beef stock**

YORKSHIRE PUDDINGS
- ☐ ^{3}/$_4$ **cup (80 g) all-purpose flour**
- ☐ **freshly ground black pepper**
- ☐ **1 egg, lightly beaten**
- ☐ **4 tablespoons milk**
- ☐ **3 tablespoons water**
- ☐ 1^1/$_2$ **tablespoons beef dripping**

HORSERADISH CREAM
- ☐ ^{1}/$_2$ **cup (120 mL) heavy cream**
- ☐ **1 tablespoon prepared horseradish**
- ☐ **freshly ground black pepper**

1   Place beef in a roasting pan, fat side up. Spread with butter and pour over 2 tablespoons oil. Bake for 30 minutes, basting with juices every 10 minutes. Heat remaining oil in another roasting pan on top of the stove and cook potatoes until brown on all sides.

2   When beef has cooked for 30 minutes, place roasting pan with potatoes on top shelf of oven and place carrots, onions and parsnips around beef. Cook for 15 minutes then turn vegetables over. Baste beef and vegetables with pan juices and cook for 15 minutes longer. Season to taste with black pepper and pour in stock. Increase oven temperature to 425°F (220°C) and cook for 15 minutes longer for rare beef, or 30 minutes longer for medium-rare beef. Transfer to a serving platter and allow to rest in a warm place before carving. Reserve roasting pan and juices.

3   To make Yorkshire Puddings, sift flour into a bowl. Add black pepper to taste and make a well in the centre. Combine egg, milk and water and pour into flour mixture. Beat slowly to incorporate wet ingredients into dry ingredients. Place 1 teaspoon beef dripping in each of six muffin pans and heat in oven until dripping is sizzling. Divide pudding batter between muffin pans and cook at 425°F (220°C) for 10-15 minutes, or until puffed and golden.

4   Take reserved roasting pan and skim fat off pan juices. Heat gently on top of stove, stirring to scrape up caramelized juices. Add extra stock or water if required and cook until reduced to a sauce consistency. Pour into a sauce boat and set aside to keep warm.

5   To make Horseradish Cream, whip cream until soft peaks form. Fold in horseradish and season with black pepper.

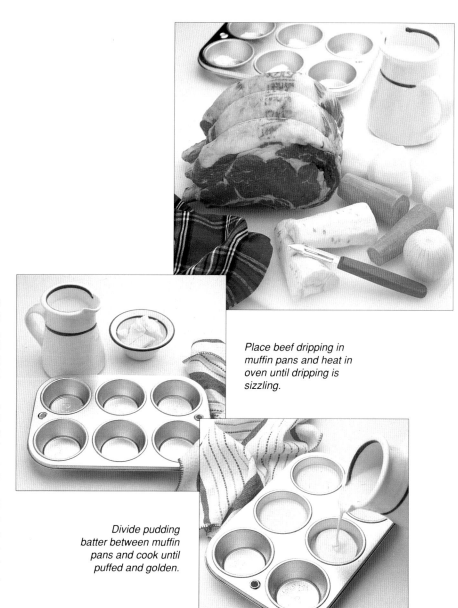

Place beef dripping in muffin pans and heat in oven until dripping is sizzling.

Divide pudding batter between muffin pans and cook until puffed and golden.

59

OUTDOOR PLEASURES

Use any excuse that occurs to you, pack all you need – good food, plates, mugs and silverware, cushions and folding chairs – and take off for a wonderful picnic or barbecue away from home.

LOBSTER TAILS WITH PISTACHIO BUTTER

There is something wonderfully extravagant and primitive about grilling lobster outdoors. If your outdoor party is by the sea, all the better.

Serves 6

- ☐ **6 uncooked lobster tails**

PISTACHIO BUTTER
- ☐ **13 tablespoons butter, softened**
- ☐ **3 tablespoons chopped, shelled, unsalted pistachios**
- ☐ **2 tablespoons finely chopped fresh parsley**
- ☐ **1 tablespoon finely snipped fresh chives**
- ☐ **1 teaspoon lemon juice**
- ☐ **1 tablespoon finely chopped fresh sage**
- ☐ **freshly ground black pepper**

1   To make Pistachio Butter, place butter in a small bowl and beat until soft and smooth. Add pistachios, parsley, chives, sage, lemon juice, and black pepper to taste and mix to combine.
2   Spread each lobster tail with a little butter mixture and place on a hot grill or under a hot broiler. Cook for 5-10 minutes, or until cooked through, turning once and basting frequently with butter during cooking. Serve topped with remaining butter.

POTATO AND DILL SALAD

A luscious rich potato salad that goes well with barbecued lobster or any grilled meats.

Serves 6-8

- ☐ **2 pounds (1 kg) new potatoes**
- ☐ **3 green onions, sliced**
- ☐ **2 tablespoons finely chopped fresh dill**
- ☐ **1 cup (240 mL) sour cream**

VINAIGRETTE
- ☐ **2 teaspoons Dijon mustard**
- ☐ **1^1/2 tablespoons white wine vinegar**
- ☐ **^{1}/2 cup (120 mL) olive oil**
- ☐ **freshly ground black pepper**

1   Boil or microwave potatoes until just tender. Drain and refresh under cold running water. Drain again and cut potatoes in half. Place in a bowl. Add green onions and dill and toss to combine.
2   To make Vinaigrette, place mustard, vinegar, oil, and black pepper to taste in a food processor or blender and process until combined. Pour over warm potatoes, add sour cream and toss gently to coat potatoes. Transfer to a serving bowl and serve at room temperature.

Lobster Tails with Pistachio Butter, Potato and Dill Salad

SMOKED CHICKEN SALAD WITH GINGER DRESSING

A pretty salad with a fresh taste that is easy to make and travels well. Put the salad in the serving bowl to marinate on the way to your picnic.

Serves 6

- [ ] **1 smoked chicken, $2^1/2$-$3^1/2$ pounds (1-1.5 kg), meat removed and broken into bite-size pieces**
- [ ] **4 green onions, finely chopped**
- [ ] **1 small red pepper, finely sliced**
- [ ] **1 small red chilli, seeded and finely sliced**
- [ ] **1 tablespoon chopped fresh coriander**
- [ ] **1 tablespoon chopped fresh mint**
- [ ] **freshly ground black pepper**

ORANGE AND GINGER DRESSING
- [ ] **3 tablespoons olive oil**
- [ ] **2 tablespoons white wine vinegar**
- [ ] **2 tablespoons freshly squeezed orange juice**
- [ ] **1 teaspoon wholegrain mustard**
- [ ] **1 teaspoon brown sugar**
- [ ] **1 teaspoon finely grated fresh ginger**

1   Place chicken, green onions, red pepper, chilli, coriander and mint in a serving bowl. Season to taste with black pepper.

2   To make dressing, place oil, vinegar, orange juice, mustard, sugar and ginger in a screwtop jar and shake well to combine. Pour over chicken mixture and toss to combine. Cover and refrigerate.

BAKED CAMEMBERT AND GORGONZOLA LOAF

Bake this loaf within the hour before you leave for your picnic. It is wrapped in foil and will stay warm.

Serves 6
Oven temperature 350°F (180°C)

- [ ] **9-inch (23 cm) round loaf of bread**
- [ ] **13 oz (375 g) Camembert cheese, sliced thinly**
- [ ] **7 oz (200 g) Gorgonzola cheese, sliced thinly**
- [ ] **3 pears, peeled, cored and sliced thinly**
- [ ] **3 fresh dates, thinly sliced**

1   Slice top from bread and scoop out centre, leaving a 1-inch (2.5 cm) shell. Top and centre of bread can be reserved and made into breadcrumbs for use later.

2   Place a layer of Camembert cheese slices over base of bread and top with a layer of Gorgonzola cheese and a layer of pear slices. Repeat layers, finishing with a layer of pears. Wrap loaf in a sheet of aluminum foil and bake for 30 minutes.

3   Remove from oven, open foil and top with dates. Rewrap while still hot for transportation to picnic. Serve directly from the foil.

BROWNIES

Dense rich chocolate brownies studded with walnuts and topped with rich chocolate icing are the perfect sweet finish to any barbecue or picnic.

Makes 24
Oven temperature 350°F (180°C)

- [ ] **$4^1/2$ oz (125 g) semi-sweet chocolate, roughly chopped**
- [ ] **9 tablespoons unsalted butter, roughly chopped**
- [ ] **1 teaspoon vanilla extract**
- [ ] **2 eggs**
- [ ] **1 cup (240 mL) sugar**
- [ ] **1 cup (240 mL) all-purpose flour**
- [ ] **$1/4$ teaspoon baking powder**
- [ ] **1 cup (240 mL) walnuts, chopped**

CHOCOLATE FUDGE ICING
- [ ] **7 oz (200 g) semi-sweet chocolate, melted**
- [ ] **3 tablespoons butter, melted**

1   Melt chocolate and butter in a saucepan over a low heat, taking care not to overheat. Remove from heat and stir in vanilla.

2   Beat eggs and sugar together until thick and creamy. Fold through chocolate mixture. Sift flour and baking powder over chocolate mixture. Sprinkle walnuts over chocolate mixture, then fold in using a spatula.

3   Spoon into a greased and lined 8-inch (20 cm) square shallow cake pan. Smooth top using spatula. Bake for 25-30 minutes, or until only just set. Cool in pan on a wire rack.

4   To make icing, combine chocolate and butter in a mixing bowl and beat until well blended. Spread over brownie and set aside to firm. Cut into squares to serve.

Smoked Chicken Salad with Ginger Dressing, Baked Camembert and Gorgonzola Loaf, Brownies

GOOSE LIVER TERRINE WITH BLUEBERRIES

Coarsely textured, this terrine is packed with strong, distinctive flavors. Serve with crusty bread, a salad and fresh fruit for a complete outdoor meal.

Serves 6
Oven temperature 400°F (200°C)

- [ ] **1 pound 10 oz (750 g) fresh goose livers (duck or chicken livers can be substituted), cleaned**
- [ ] **freshly ground black pepper**
- [ ] **$^1/_4$ teaspoon nutmeg**
- [ ] **$^1/_4$ teaspoon Chinese five spice powder**
- [ ] **$^1/_4$ teaspoon sugar**
- [ ] **4 tablespoons sherry**
- [ ] **8 very thin slices prosciutto or bacon**
- [ ] **4 slices lean bacon, chopped**
- [ ] **18 oz (500 g) ground pork**
- [ ] **$^3/_4$ cup (180 mL) white wine**
- [ ] **16 oz (440 g) fresh or canned blueberries, drained**
- [ ] **2 bay leaves**

1   Place livers in a bowl and cover with lukewarm water. Set aside to soak for 1 hour.

2   Drain livers and place in a clean bowl. Add black pepper to taste, nutmeg, five spice powder, sugar and sherry. Toss to combine all ingredients. Cover with plastic wrap and refrigerate for 4 hours.

3   Line a greased 9 x 4-inch (23 x 10 cm) terrine or loaf dish with prosciutto or bacon allowing slices to overhang the top. Grind one-third of marinated livers with bacon allowing slices to overhang the top. Combine with pork and wine, and season to taste with black pepper. Spread one-third of this mixture into base of terrine. Top with half the remaining livers and scatter with half the blueberries. Cover with another one-third of the ground mixture. Cover with a slice of prosciutto or bacon and fold overhanging slices into the center to cover the filling. Top with remaining blueberries, then another layer of livers, finally finishing with remaining minced mixture. Place bay leaves on top and cover tightly with lid or foil.

4   Place in a baking dish with enough hot water to come halfway up sides of dish and cook for $1^1/_2$-$1^3/_4$ hours, or until mixture is coming away from sides of dish and is brown around edges.

5   Remove lid, drain off excess liquid and set aside to cool. To serve, turn out and cut into even slices.

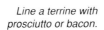
Line a terrine with prosciutto or bacon.

Grind one-third of livers with bacon, combine with pork and wine and season with black pepper.

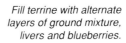
Fill terrine with alternate layers of ground mixture, livers and blueberries.

NAUGHTY BUT NICE

What could be more indulgent than Passion Fruit Petits Fours! Try Cheese Cigars with Coriander Pesto as a tasty pre-dinner treat. For those who really want the ultimate indulgence, see the Master Class and make the Surprise Truffle Bag.

❦

SPUN SUGAR TOPPED MINIATURE PARIS BREST

Choux pastry is easy to make. Just remember, do not tip the flour in before the water mixture is boiling and do not add all the eggs at once.

Makes 18
Oven temperature 425°F (220°C)

CHOUX PASTRY
- [ ] **1 cup (240 mL) water**
- [ ] **5 tablespoons butter, cut into small pieces**
- [ ] **³/4 cup (180 mL) all-purpose flour, sifted**
- [ ] **3 eggs**

FILLING
- [ ] **1 cup (240 mL) heavy cream, whipped**
- [ ] **9 oz (250 g) diced fresh fruits**

SPUN SUGAR
- [ ] **1 cup (240 mL) sugar**
- [ ] **4 tablespoons water**
- [ ] **confectioners sugar for dusting**

1   To make pastry, place water and butter in a saucepan and slowly bring to the boil. As soon as the mixture boils, quickly stir in flour, using a wooden spoon. Cook over a low heat, stirring constantly for 2 minutes, or until mixture is smooth and leaves sides of pan. Remove from heat and set aside to cool slightly. Beat in eggs, one at a time, beating well after each addition and until mixture is light and glossy.

2   Line baking trays with parchment paper and trace 2-inch (5 cm) circles on it. Spoon pastry mixture into a piping bag fitted with a ¹/2-inch (1 cm) plain nozzle. Pipe two rows of pastry, one on top of the other, inside the traced circles. Bake for 8 minutes. Prop open oven door using the handle of a wooden spoon and cook pastries for 10 minutes longer, or until golden and crisp. Remove from tray and cool on a wire rack. Split pastries in half, using a bread knife. Return to the oven and bake at 250°F (120°C) for 5 minutes or until pastries dry out.

3   Fill bottom halves with whipped cream and top with fruit. Replace lids and set aside.

4   To make spun sugar, place sugar and water in a small saucepan. Cook over a medium heat stirring constantly until sugar dissolves. Continue to cook without stirring until mixture is golden. Remove from heat and stand until bubbles subside. Spin sugar and decorate pastries. Serve within an hour.

Spun Sugar Topped Miniature Paris Brest

CHEESE CIGARS WITH CORIANDER PESTO

A pesto made of coriander is the perfect accompaniment to these tasty Cheese Cigars – serve as an indulgent snack or as a pre-dinner treat.

Makes 12

- ☐ **12 slices white sandwich bread, crusts removed**
- ☐ **2 teaspoons prepared English mustard**
- ☐ **4 tablespoons finely grated fresh Parmesan cheese**
- ☐ **^{1}/2 cup (120 mL) grated mozzarella cheese**
- ☐ **1 tablespoon snipped fresh chives**
- ☐ **cayenne pepper**
- ☐ **1 egg, lightly beaten**
- ☐ **vegetable oil for cooking**

CORIANDER PESTO
- ☐ **3 large bunches fresh coriander**
- ☐ **2 cloves garlic, crushed**
- ☐ **60 g pine nuts**

- ☐ **^{1}/2 cup (120 mL) olive oil**
- ☐ **^{2}/3 cup (160 mL) grated fresh Parmesan cheese**

1 Roll each slice of bread with a rolling pin, to flatten as much as possible.
2 Combine mustard, Parmesan cheese, mozzarella cheese, chives, and cayenne pepper to taste in a bowl. Divide mixture between bread slices and spread over half of each bread slice. Brush unspread sides of bread slices with egg. Roll each slice up tightly using the egg to seal rolls. Arrange side by side on a tray. Cover and refrigerate until ready to cook.
3 Heat ^{3}/4-inch (2 cm) of oil in a skillet. When hot, cook cigars a few at a time until evenly golden all over. Drain on paper towels.
4 To make pesto, place coriander leaves, garlic and pine nuts in a food processor or blender and process until finely chopped. With machine running slowly, pour in oil and process mixture until smooth. Add cheese and process to blend. Serve with hot cigars.

CHOCOLATE PASTILLES WITH FRUITS AND NUTS

Makes 32

- ☐ **9 oz (250 g) semi-sweet chocolate, melted and cooled slightly**
- ☐ **^{1}/2 cup (120 mL) dried papaya pieces**
- ☐ **^{1}/2 cup (120 mL) dried banana chips**
- ☐ **16 candied cherries, quartered**
- ☐ **3 tablespoons sliced almonds**

1 Line two oven trays with wax paper. Drop spoonfuls of melted chocolate onto trays leaving 4 inches (10 cm) between each. Quickly spread each spoonful into a flat disk using the back of a spoon. Stick papaya, banana chips, cherries and almonds upright in chocolate and refrigerate until set.
2 Carefully remove pastilles from paper using a spatula. Store in airtight containers.

DOUBLE-INDULGENT FUDGE

Layered fudge studded with nuts – each piece an indulgence.

Makes 32

DARK CHOCOLATE LAYER
- ☐ **14 oz (400 g) semi-sweet chocolate**
- ☐ **5^1/2 oz (155 g) sweetened condensed milk**
- ☐ **2 tablespoons butter**
- ☐ **2 tablespoons brandy**
- ☐ **^{1}/2 cup (120 mL) blanched almonds, roughly chopped and toasted**

WHITE CHOCOLATE LAYER
- ☐ **14 oz (400 g) white chocolate**
- ☐ **5^1/2 oz (155 g) sweetened condensed milk**
- ☐ **2 tablespoons butter**
- ☐ **2 tablespoons Baileys Irish Cream**
- ☐ **^{1}/2 cup (120 mL) hazelnuts, toasted peeled and roughly chopped**

1 To make Dark Chocolate Layer, place semi-sweet chocolate, condensed milk, butter and brandy in a saucepan and cook over a low heat, stirring constantly, until mixture is smooth and well combined. Fold in almonds and pour mixture into an 8-inch (20 cm) square greased and foil-lined cake pan. Refrigerate until firm.
2 To make White Chocolate Layer, place

white chocolate, condensed milk, butter and Baileys in a saucepan and cook over a low heat, stirring constantly, until mixture is smooth and well combined. Fold in hazelnuts and spread mixture over Dark Chocolate Layer. Refrigerate until firm. To serve, cut into pieces.

❧

PASSION FRUIT PETITS FOURS

Tiny butterfly cakes flavored with passion fruit are an impressive finish.

Makes 40
Oven temperature 350°F (180°C)

- ☐ **3 tablespoons butter**
- ☐ **1 teaspoon Grand Marnier**
- ☐ **2 tablespoons sugar**
- ☐ **1 egg**
- ☐ **²/₃ cup (160 mL) self-rising flour, sifted**
- ☐ **3 tablespoons passion fruit pulp**

TOPPING
- ☐ **¹/₂ cup (120 mL) cream, whipped**
- ☐ **2 tablespoons passion fruit pulp**
- ☐ **2 tablespoons confectioners sugar, sifted**

1 Place butter and Grand Marnier in a bowl and beat until creamy. Add sugar and continue beating until light and fluffy.
2 Add eggs one at a time, beating well after each addition. Fold in flour alternately with passion fruit pulp.
3 Spoon mixture into petit four paper cases, placed on an oven tray. Bake for 6-8 minutes, or until cooked through

*Left: Cheese Cigars with Coriander Pesto
Above: Chocolate Pastilles with Fruits and Nuts, Double-Indulgent Fudge, Passion Fruit Petits Fours*

and golden. Remove from oven and set aside to cool.
4 To assemble, cut a slice from top of each cake. Halve each slice and set aside. Place cream in a piping bag fitted with a small star nozzle. Pipe top of cake with cream, position tops at an angle, back to back, in cream. Top with a little passion fruit pulp and dust lightly with confectioners sugar.

M A S T E R C L A S S

SURPRISE TRUFFLE BAG

A marzipan bag filled with chocolate truffles – what more spectacular way could there be to end a special dinner?

Serves 12

- ☐ **cocoa, sifted**
- ☐ **1¹/₃ pounds (600 g) marzipan**
- ☐ **1 egg white, lightly beaten**
- ☐ **2 yards (2 m) thin ribbon**

RICH COCONUT TRUFFLES
- ☐ **4 tablespoons sweetened condensed milk**
- ☐ **³/₄ cup (180 mL) shredded coconut**
- ☐ **1 tablespoon coconut flavored liqueur**
- ☐ **7 oz (200 g) semi-sweet chocolate**

BRANDY TRUFFLES
- ☐ **7 oz (200 g) milk chocolate, roughly chopped**
- ☐ **2 tablespoons cream**
- ☐ **2 tablespoons unsalted butter**
- ☐ **3 teaspoons brandy**
- ☐ **cocoa, sifted**

WHITE PRALINE TRUFFLES
- ☐ **7 oz (200 g) white chocolate, roughly chopped**
- ☐ **2 tablespoons cream**
- ☐ **2 tablespoons unsalted butter**
- ☐ **¹/₃ cup (80 mL) sugar**
- ☐ **3 tablespoons water**
- ☐ **¹/₄ cup (60 mL) slivered almonds**
- ☐ **confectioners sugar, sifted**

1　To make Rich Coconut Truffles, combine condensed milk, coconut and liqueur in a bowl and mix to combine. Refrigerate until firm. Roll spoonfuls of mixture into small balls and dip in melted chocolate to coat. Place on a foil-lined tray and set aside until chocolate is firm.

2　To make Brandy Truffles, place milk chocolate, cream and butter in top of a double boiler and cook over simmering water, stirring, until chocolate melts and mixture is well combined. Stir in brandy. Refrigerate until firm. Roll spoonfuls of mixture into small balls and roll in cocoa. Refrigerate until required.

3　To make White Praline Truffles, place white chocolate, cream and butter in top of a double boiler and cook over simmering water, stirring, until chocolate melts and mixture is well combined. Place sugar and water in a saucepan and cook over a medium heat, stirring constantly until sugar

dissolves. Bring to the boil and continue to cook, without stirring, until golden brown. Place almonds on a greased cookie sheet and pour caramel over. Set aside to cool. Place caramel in a food processor and process until finely chopped, but not powdered. Fold into chocolate. Refrigerate until firm. Roll spoonfuls into small balls and roll in confectioners sugar. Refrigerate until required.

4　To make marzipan bag, dust work surface with cocoa and knead marzipan with a little egg white until it is smooth and pliable and an even chocolate color.

5　Roll out marzipan as thinly as possible on a cocoa-dusted surface to form a large round. Place truffles in a pile in centre of marzipan and gently bring up sides of marzipan to form a neat bag. Tie with a ribbon.

Dust work surface with sifted cocoa and knead marzipan with a little egg white until smooth, and an even chocolate color.

Roll out marzipan on a cocoa-dusted surface to form a large round.

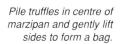

Pile truffles in centre of marzipan and gently lift sides to form a bag.

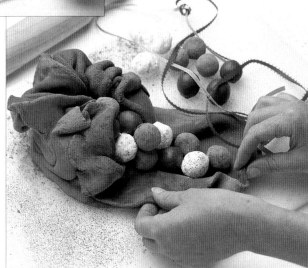

FIERY FINISHES

Flambé food is a dramatic and magnificent touch to any meal. But remember that special care is required – both in the kitchen and at the table. The flame under the pan should not be too high and you should use only a small quantity of alcohol at a time.

FLAMBE OF EXOTIC FRUITS

Use a variety of luscious fresh fruits to create an irresistible finale to your meal!

Choose from any of the following fruits:
- [ ] **pineapple and melon wedges**
- [ ] **kiwi fruit, peeled and cut into long quarters**
- [ ] **bananas, peeled and cut into 4-6 pieces**
- [ ] **apricots, pitted and cut into quarters**
- [ ] **mandarin and orange segments**
- [ ] **seedless grapes**
- [ ] **whole strawberries**
- [ ] **small bowl of alcohol of your choice, such as rum, brandy, Grand Marnier, Kirsch, Curacao or Cointreau**
- [ ] **bowl of brown sugar**
- [ ] **bowls of whipped cream**

Arrange fruit on a large platter. Each person secures a piece of fruit on a fork and dips the fruit into alcohol, then sugar and holds it over a fondue flame. When fruit caramelizes, dip into cream and eat at once.

Alternative Method
1   Sprinkle fruit with sugar and dot with butter. Place fruit in a heavy-based skillet and cook quickly until sugar melts and sauce bubbles.
2   Warm alcohol in a small saucepan, ignite and pour over fruit, shaking pan gently. Serve at once with whipped cream.

Flambé of Exotic Fruits

China Limoges

FLAMBE MANGOES OVER VANILLA ICE CREAM

The special combination of sweet juicy mangoes, sugar and Kirsch make up this light summery dessert. Make your own ice cream, or buy one of the specialty brands now available, to complete this delicious dessert.

Serves 4

- [ ] vanilla ice cream
- [ ] 4 tablespoons sugar
- [ ] 2 tablespoons Kirsch (cherry brandy)
- [ ] 2 large ripe mangoes, pitted, peeled and sliced

1   Spoon 4 large scoops of vanilla ice cream into four individual heatproof glass dishes. Keep chilled.

2   Place a large, heavy-based skillet over a medium heat for 2 minutes. Add sugar and melt without stirring until it begins to caramelize. Stir until sugar is evenly caramelized.

3   Add Kirsch and ignite immediately.

Quickly stir in mangoes and cook until flames die and mangoes are heated through.

4   Spoon hot mangoes and juices over chilled ice cream. Serve immediately.

FLAMED KIDNEYS WITH RED WINE

Serve this robust dish with hot, buttery noodles and a green salad.

Serves 4

- [ ] 1^1/2 pounds (750 g) lambs' kidneys, trimmed and halved
- [ ] 2 tablespoons seasoned flour
- [ ] 9 tablespoons butter
- [ ] 9 oz (250 g) small white mushrooms, halved
- [ ] 1 teaspoon lemon juice
- [ ] 2 tablespoons brandy
- [ ] ^{1}/2 cup (120 mL) red wine
- [ ] freshly ground black pepper
- [ ] 1 tablespoon finely chopped fresh parsley

1   Place kidneys in lightly salted water

and set aside to soak for 10 minutes. Drain, pat dry and chop coarsely. Toss kidneys in seasoned flour to coat.

2   Melt 6 tablespoons butter in a skillet and cook kidneys for 3 minutes over a medium-high heat, stirring with a wooden spoon. Remove kidneys, using a slotted spoon, and set aside.

3   Melt remaining butter in same skillet and cook mushrooms, stirring, for 4 minutes. Add lemon juice and cook until mushrooms give up most of their juices.

4   Return kidneys and any juices to skillet, toss to combine, then remove from heat. Add brandy and ignite immediately. When flames die, return skillet to heat and add wine. Turn heat to medium-low and cook until kidneys are tender but still pink. Season to taste with black pepper. Sprinkle with parsley and serve immediately.

COGNAC LOBSTERS WITH BASIL BUTTER

Sizzling lobster flambéed with cognac then topped with a fresh herb butter makes for a wonderfully easy and very indulgent meal.

Serves 4

- ☐ **2 pounds (900 g) uncooked lobsters, halved and cleaned**
- ☐ **2 tablespoons lemon juice**
- ☐ **2 tablespoons olive oil**
- ☐ **freshly ground black pepper**

BASIL BUTTER
- ☐ **9 tablespoons butter, roughly chopped**
- ☐ **2 tablespoons finely chopped fresh basil leaves**
- ☐ **2 teaspoons finely chopped fresh parsley**
- ☐ **freshly ground black pepper**

- ☐ **3 tablespoons cognac**

1   To make Basil Butter, beat butter until smooth. Stir in basil and parsley and season to taste with black pepper. Place in a small bowl and refrigerate until required.

2   Drizzle lobsters with lemon juice and brush flesh with oil. Cook under a hot broiler or on a grill, shell side first, for 5 minutes. Turn over and cook for 5-10 minutes, or until flesh is just cooked. Brush with extra oil, if necessary, during cooking.

3   Remove lobsters from heat. Remove flesh from tails in one piece and cut into pieces. Pile back into shells and set aside to keep warm. Warm cognac, hold a lighted match over it and as soon as it ignites spoon over lobster.

4   Divide butter into four portions and place one piece on each lobster half. Serve immediately.

FLAMBE TIPS

❦ Alcohol must be warmed to flame effectively, however, if overheated the alcohol will evaporate before it flames.

❦ The flaming alcohol will help burn away excessive fats, dissolve the crust at the bottom of the pan and form a glaze that can become the basis of a sauce.

❦ A sprinkling of a little sugar over the food just before flaming will produce a longer lasting flame.

❦ Gently shaking the pan when the flame has been ignited will distribute both flame and alcohol, and therefore the flavor, over the food.

Left: Flambé Mangoes over Vanilla Ice Cream
Below: Flamed Kidneys with Red Wine, Cognac Lobsters with Basil Butter

PAMPERED PANTRY

Balsamic Vinegar

Balsamic vinegar is produced from the not yet fully fermented new red wine of the season. It is aged in wooden barrels to give it a distinctive almost sweet flavor and it is especially suitable for making a vinaigrette. Like any good quality vinegar, it should be transparent, not 'cloudy'. Because of its sweet flavor, balsamic vinegar is also used to dress fresh fruits and berries. In Italy well-matured balsamic vinegar is sometimes drunk as an after-dinner liqueur.

Sun-Dried Tomatoes

Usually bottled, and packed in olive oil, these richly flavored tomatoes will enhance almost any dish that requires the use of fresh tomatoes – salads, casseroles and pizza toppings. Sun-dried tomatoes once opened are best stored in the refrigerator.

Couverture

This refers to the chocolate coating or covering that is used for confectionery, cakes and biscuits. It is made from chocolate that has a high proportion of cocoa butter – the higher the content of cocoa butter, the richer and creamier the chocolate. Couverture can be used to cover a special gâteau and for making homemade chocolates and confectionery. As it does not require tempering it is easier to use than ordinary chocolate. Couverture is available from specialty food stores.

Oils

Studies have shown the link between heart disease and the consumption of large amounts of solid animal fats. In the interest of healthier living, the use of oils for cooking and food preparation has recently been promoted. There are many types of oils – derived from seeds, fruits and nuts. Each has its own distinctive flavor, so experiment to find those that you like best.

Sesame seed oil has a light, distinctive flavor especially suitable for Eastern dishes.

Olive oil is available in three grades: Extra Virgin, Virgin and Fine (pure). The color ranges from thick and green, to pale and yellow. Olive oil can be used for general cooking and is popular in salad.

Nut oils such as walnut, hazelnut and almond are more expensive but their flavor is superb, and when used as the base of a vinaigrette for salad the flavor is marvelous.

Olives

Traditionally grown in the Mediterranean region, olives are now grown successfully in other parts of the world. Olives are either green (unripened) or black (ripened). Green olives are preserved in a soda solution and then pickled in brine. Black olives are preserved in brine or olive oil. Olives can be stuffed – most commonly with red pimentos or almonds. They are an excellent addition to salads, casseroles, cheese plates, hors d'oeuvres and antipasto platters. Store olives away from direct heat and light and serve at room temperature for the best flavor. After opening, store in the refrigerator.

Wild Rice

This dark brown to black grain with a nutty flavor is the seed from a type of grass that grows in swamp areas of the United States and Canada. Because the habitat in which it grows is isolated, harvesting is difficult – this is reflected in its high price. Wild rice can be mixed with white and brown rice, making an eye-catching salad or tasty accompaniment.

Dried Mushrooms

These can be used in a similar way as fresh mushrooms, however, they require a little more preparation and cooking. Unlike the fresh variety that will keep for only a few days, dried mushrooms keep for months. When reconstituted, approximately 1 oz (30 g) will provide the equivalent of 9 oz (250 g) fresh mushrooms. Dried mushrooms require 15-30 minutes soaking in water before use.

There are many varieties available and they can be used as a vegetable in stir-fries, as an ingredient in a meat or poultry stuffing, or in soups.

Coconut Milk

Coconut milk and cream of coconut are used in the preparation of curries, satay sauces, authentic Thai, Indian and Asian dishes, and give texture and flavor. You might also like to try them instead of cow's milk when baking coconut biscuits. Once opened, canned coconut milk and cream of coconut will keep in the refrigerator for only a day or two.

Coconut milk and cream of coconut are interchangeable and it is easy to make your own. To make coconut milk, place 18 oz (500 g) of shredded coconut in a bowl and add 3 cups (705 mL) of boiling water. Leave to stand for 30 minutes, and strain through muslin, squeezing the coconut to extract as much liquid as possible. This will give a thick coconut milk or cream. The coconut can be used again to make a weaker coconut milk.

Liqueurs

The addition of a liqueur to sauces, marinades and desserts will make them just that bit more delicious. Brandy liqueurs, Grand Marnier, Cointreau, Calvados, and Amaretto all give delicious flavors. The miniature bottles now readily available in most liquor stores will mean that an extensive array can be amassed for a reasonable price.

USEFUL INFORMATION

In this book, ingredients such as fish and meat are given in ounces and grams so you know how much to buy. A small inexpensive set of kitchen scales is always handy and very easy to use. Other ingredients in our recipes are given in tablespoons and cups, so you will need a set of measuring cups (1 cup, $^1/_2$ cup, $^1/_3$ cup and $^1/_4$ cup), a set of measuring spoons (1 tablespoon, 1 teaspoon, $^1/_2$ teaspoon and $^1/_4$ teaspoon) and a transparent graduated measuring cup (1 cup or 250 mL) for measuring liquids. Cup and spoon measures are level.

OVEN TEMPERATURES

°C	°F
120	250
140	275
150	300
160	325
180	350
190	375
200	400
220	425
240	475
250	500

QUICK CONVERTER

Metric	Imperial
5 mm	$^1/_4$ in
1 cm	$^1/_2$ in
2 cm	$^3/_4$ in
2.5 cm	1 in
5 cm	2 in
10 cm	4 in
15 cm	6 in
20 cm	8 in
23 cm	9 in
25 cm	10 in
30 cm	12 in

MEASURING DRY INGREDIENTS

Metric	Imperial
15 g	$^1/_2$ oz
30 g	1 oz
60 g	2 oz
90 g	3 oz
125 g	4 oz
155 g	5 oz
185 g	6 oz
220 g	7 oz
250 g	8 oz
280 g	9 oz
315 g	10 oz
375 g	12 oz
410 g	13 oz
440 g	14 oz
470 g	15 oz
500 g	16 oz (1 lb)
750 g	1 lb 8 oz
1 kg	2 lb
1.5 kg	3 lb

MEASURING LIQUIDS

Metric	Imperial	Cup
30 mL	1 fl oz	
60 mL	2 fl oz	$^1/_4$ cup
90 mL	3 fl oz	
120 mL	4 fl oz	$^1/_2$ cup
155 mL	5 fl oz	
170 mL	$5^1/_2$ fl oz	$^2/_3$ cup
185 mL	6 fl oz	
220 mL	7 fl oz	
240 mL	8 fl oz	1 cup
470 mL	16 fl oz	2 cups
600 mL	20 fl oz (1 pt)	
750 mL	$1^1/_4$ pt	
1 litre	$1^3/_4$ pt	4 cups
1.2 litres	2 pt	

METRIC CUPS & SPOONS

Metric	Cups	Imperial
60 mL	$^1/_4$ cup	2 fl oz
80 mL	$^1/_3$ cup	$2^1/_2$ fl oz
120 mL	$^1/_2$ cup	4 fl oz
240 mL	1 cup	8 fl oz
	Spoons	
1.25 mL	$^1/_4$ teaspoon	
2.5 mL	$^1/_2$ teaspoon	
5 mL	1 teaspoon	
15 mL	1 tablespoon	

INDEX

ACKNOWLEDGEMENTS
The publishers wish to thank the following Admiral Appliances; Black & Decker (Australasia) Pty Ltd; Blanco Appliances; Knebel Kitchens; Leigh Mardon Pty Ltd; Master Foods of Australia; Meadow Lea Foods; Namco Cookware; Ricegrowers' Co-op Mills Ltd; Sunbeam Corporation Ltd; Tycraft Pty Ltd distributors of Braun, Australia; White Wings Foods for their assistance during recipe testing.

Penny Cook for her assistance during recipe testing.

COVER
Ashley Mackevicius (photography), Wendy Berecry (Styling). Plates and cup from Royal Doulton.